Where to place the grace note?

*Conversations on Classical Piano Music
with Yu Chun Yee*

Where to place the grace note?

Conversations on Classical Piano Music with Yu Chun Yee

Lin Li

 **World Scientific**

NEW JERSEY · LONDON · SINGAPORE · BEIJING · SHANGHAI · HONG KONG · TAIPEI · CHENNAI · TOKYO

Published by

World Scientific Publishing Co. Pte. Ltd.
5 Toh Tuck Link, Singapore 596224
USA office: 27 Warren Street, Suite 401-402, Hackensack, NJ 07601
UK office: 57 Shelton Street, Covent Garden, London WC2H 9HE

British Library Cataloguing-in-Publication Data
A catalogue record for this book is available from the British Library.

WHERE TO PLACE THE GRACE NOTE?
Conversations on Classical Piano Music with Yu Chun Yee

ISBN 978-981-120-704-4
ISBN 978-981-120-770-9 (pbk)

For any available supplementary material, please visit
https://www.worldscientific.com/worldscibooks/10.1142/11466#t=suppl

Typeset by Stallion Press
Email: enquiries@stallionpress.com

Printed in Singapore

Contents

Acknowledgments

I wish to thank World Scientific for the opportunity to finally put these conversations in print. Special thanks to Prof K K Phua for his generosity and trust right from the start, and to Sandhya for her patience with the proofs.

This book has been written across many different spaces — Cambridge, Singapore, Leuven, Zoersel, Riyadh — in good company and laughter. I would like to thank my friends and families for their support and advice throughout this project, especially those who took the time to review and comment on the first chapter.

And finally I would like to thank my husband, Stijn, for giving me much courage and happiness.

Music Cited

A Spotify playlist with the music cited is available at https://open. spotify.com/playlist/18J6uMeMxbZsEbBVxaZN0c. In cases where the complete work consists of many parts (for instance the piano sonatas or the "Goldberg Variations") I have only included the first movement or the first variation. The entire work can be accessed by clicking on the album from which the recording has been extracted.

Introduction

Copland, "Hoe-Down" and "Saturday Night Waltz" from *Rodeo*

Fauré, Nocturne No. 4 in E-flat Major, op. 36

Liszt, Piano Sonata in B Minor, S. 178

Schubert, Piano Sonata in A Minor, D. 784

Chapter 1

Mozart, Piano Sonata in C Major, K.279

> 0:52-1:06 of the recording (Mitsuko Uchida, *Piano Sonatas Nos. 1, 14 & 18; Fantasia in C Minor,* Decca, 1985) corresponds to the music printed in Fig. 2.

Bach, "Goldberg Variations", BWV 988 performed by Glenn Gould, Igor Levit, András Schiff, and Landowska

Bach, Double Violin Concerto in D Minor, BWV 1043

Chapter 2

Chopin, Nocturne in G Minor, op. 37 no. 1

> 0:00-0:20 of the recording (Claudio Arrau, *Chopin: The Nocturnes*, Philips, 1978) corresponds to the first four phrases highlighted in Fig. 5.

Chopin, *Funeral March* from Piano Sonata No. 2 in B-flat Minor, op. 37

Chopin, 4 Impromptus for piano

Chopin, Prelude in E Minor, op. 28 no. 4

Radiohead, "Exit Music (For a Film)"

Jane Birkin and Serge Gainsbourg, "Jane B."

Antônio Carlos Jobim, Astrud Gilberto, Norman Gimbel, and Vinícius de Moraes, "How Insensitive"

Beethoven, "Moonlight Sonata", op. 27 no. 2

> 0:21 of the recording (Daniel Barenboim, *Beethoven: The Piano Sonatas*, Deutsche Grammophon, 1984) corresponds to the chord discussed in Fig. 8.

The Beatles, "Do You Want to Know a Secret"

> Neapolitan Sixth chords can be heard at 0:10 and 1:18 of the recording (*Please Please Me (Remastered)*, Calderstone Productions Limited, 1963)

Jacques Brel, "Ne Me Quitte Pas"

> A Neapolitan Sixth chord can be heard at 2:46 of the recording (*15 Ans D'Amour*, Barclay, 1988)

The Rolling Stones, "Mother's Little Helper"

> A Neapolitan Sixth chord can be heard at 0:20 of the record-ing (*Aftermath (UK version)*, ABKCO Music & Records Inc., 1966)

Schumann, *Variations on the name Abegg*, op. 1

> 7:10-7:18 of the recording (Sviatoslav Richer, *Piano Recital: The Art of Sviatoslav Richter*, Deutsche Grammophon The Rosette Collection, 1994) corresponds to the bars highlighted in Fig. 9.

Beethoven, Piano Sonata No. 4 in E-flat Major, op. 7

> 2:14-2:18 of the recording (Alfred Brendel, *Beethoven: Com-plete Piano Sonatas & Concertos*, Decca, 2010) corresponds to the boxed chords in Fig. 10.

Schubert, *Moments Musicaux*, D. 780 no. 5 in F Minor

> 0:28 of the recording (Artur Schnabel, *Schubert: 6 Moments Musicaux, D.780 & Allegretto, D. 915*, Parlophone Records Limited, 2019) corresponds to bar 34 (marked *pp*) in Fig. 11.

Schubert, Piano Sonata in A Minor, D. 784

> 0:19-0:23 of the recording (Sviatoslav Richter, *Schubert Piano Sonatas Nos. 13 & 14: Impromptus D. 899 Nos. 2 & 4*, Olympia, 1979) corresponds to the first murmur in Fig. 13.

> 0:43-0:47 of the recording (Sviatoslav Richter, *Schubert Piano Sonatas Nos. 13 & 14: Impromptus D.899 Nos. 2 & 4*, Olympia, 1979) corresponds to the second murmur in Fig. 13.

Schubert, Piano Sonata in B-flat Major, D. 960

> 0:27-0:38 of the recording (Sviatoslav Richter, *Schubert Piano Sonatas Nos. 19 & 21*, Olympia, 1973) corresponds to the murmur in Fig. 14.

Chapter 3

Chopin, Mazurka in C-sharp Minor, op. 50 no. 3 performed by Rubinstein

0:00-0:42 of the recording (Arthur Rubinstein, *Chopin Mazurkas 1938–1939*, Naxos, 2000) corresponds to the music discussed in Fig. 1.

0:43-0:51 of the recording corresponds to the music discussed in Fig. 2.

1:14-1:24 of the recording corresponds to the music discussed in Fig. 3.

Chopin, Mazurka in C-sharp Minor, op. 50 no. 3 performed by Horowitz and Fou Ts'ong

Schumann, Fantasy in C Major, op. 17

Chapter 4

Debussy, *Préludes*

Chopin, Piano Sonata No. 3 in B Minor, op. 58

Beethoven, Piano Sonata in C Minor, op. 111

Beethoven, Piano Sonata in F Minor, op. 57, "Appassionata"

Beethoven, Piano Sonata in C Major, op. 53, "Waldstein"

Chapter 5

Debussy, "Reflets dans l'Eau" from *Images*

Chapter 6

Beethoven, Piano Sonata in A Major, op. 101

Beethoven, Piano Sonata in E-flat Major, op. 81A, "Les Adieux"

Mendelssohn, *Lieder Ohne Worte,* op. 19 no. 1 in E Major

Bach, Chromatic Fantasy and Fugue in D Minor, BWV 903

Bach, Gavotte in D Minor from *English Suite* No. 6

Beethoven, Sonata in E-flat Major, op. 31 no. 3

Mendelssohn, *Variations Sérieuses,* op. 54

Liszt, *Venezia e Napoli,* S. 159

Introduction

The Call of the Orioles

I first met Prof Yu in 2009. At that time, I was a fourth-year English Literature undergraduate at the National University of Singapore, writing up a thesis on Samuel Beckett and the middle voice. I had also been part of the university's piano ensemble for four years, playing two-piano duets with my colleagues for annual concerts; I remember greatly enjoying Copland's "Hoe-Down" and "Saturday Night Waltz" from his ballet *Rodeo*. When a duet went well, you felt a great sense of synergy and energy — the laughter, excitement, and relief we shared backstage were unforgettable.

However, things on the solo piano scene were not going very well for me. I had just failed my Licentiate of the Royal Schools of Music (LRSM) in Piano Performance, greatly disappointing my previous teacher. I remember very well how I received the news. I had been notified to collect my results from the office at Victoria Concert Hall, and upon being handed a slim envelope rather than a cardboard-backed envelope (containing a certificate), I knew I must have failed again. This had happened to me for the previous exam, the DipABRSM in Piano Performance, which I had fortunately passed on the second attempt, solely on the patience of my teacher.

At that time, the old Capitol Building in Singapore had a very quaint Japanese curry restaurant, which I frequented very often. As my order of Ebi Tempura Curry arrived, I opened the envelop and realized that I had failed by more than a slight margin; in fact, I had failed all components of the exam: performance, sight-reading, viva voce. There was no redemption to be found. The playing was insecure, shaky, and lacked interpretation, the examiners said, adding that the groundwork for reliable technique was sorely missing. I remember calling my teacher to explain the situation, and he was very understanding about it. It's not a problem to fail, he said, but think about whether you want to sit for it again, and I'd call you when I have free slots in my schedule for you to come back for lessons. I put down the phone, finished my Ebi tempura and thought it really might be time for me to recognize that I could progress no further in music despite my love for it. The waiters, seeing how dejected I was, offered me a matcha ice cream.

I waited for a few months, but he never called. When I look back on this today, I choose to believe that it slipped his mind; but given the rather vulnerable state I was in, I assumed that it was his way of saying "it's time for you to move on." By this point, I had decided that I will find a way to improve my playing and sit for the exam again. It wasn't so much a stubbornness that prevailed, but desperation: I had known nothing more personal, comforting, and inspiring than music in my life, and I had to find a way to go on. I still had dreams of becoming a performer.

A good friend suggested that I contact Prof Yu. "I have no idea what he's like," he said, "but he's supposed to be very good. He might need you to audition though."

I called Prof Yu and he suggested I drop by the next day with a piece to play. "Any piece that you're confident of," he said. I spent the rest of the day at the piano, practicing Fauré's Nocturne No. 4 in E-flat Major.

Prof Yu lives in a very beautiful house set in one of Singapore's most well-preserved heritage districts. On a quiet morning, you can hear the black-naped orioles (a small beautiful yellow bird) whistling in good counterpoint to the cacophony of the roosters in the neighbor's compounds. This is a sense of tranquility that I've learnt to savor for all my remaining lessons, but on that very morning, there surely was no peace to be known.

I was led up to the third floor where Prof Yu was waiting by the piano in his study. "Right on time!" he said, looking at his clock. (I have only been late on one occasion for the next ten years, much to my regret).

To be fair, there was nothing at all menacing about Prof Yu and the surroundings I was in. He looked to be in his early 60s, wore a very kind expression, was very comfortably dressed in casual wear, and the entire studio, full of recordings, music scores and a little desk by the side, emanated a sense of calm and warmth. I looked at the Steinway that stood in the middle of the studio, adorned with even more scores around it, and at that point I truly, completely froze. You only see Steinways when you need to perform; Steinways are not friendly, as a matter of fact, the one before me now was undoubtedly a monster.

"What will you play today?" Prof Yu asked.

"Uhm, I prepared Fauré's 4th Nocturne."

"The E-flat? Beautiful. Whenever you're ready."

I placed the score on the stand and tried to get my bearings. I started playing but it seemed to me that the notes were quivering. Horrendous. I kept going; don't stop, I told myself. Things were starting to give way. My left hand wouldn't sound. Not a nocturne, a nightmare, I thought. And what's happening to my right foot? The pedals weren't working. My left foot ended up being twisted unnaturally below the bench. And gosh, there's a page turn coming up, I need to focus and get this right. Disastrous. I sound like a fool, all this perspiration too. Why is my little finger not cooperating?

"Thank you," Prof Yu said, after the last note finally sounded.

Then no one said anything.

"You do not play well. But you play with tremendous confidence."

"Yes." I said, not knowing what to say. What kind of a response is "yes"? Should I have said "thank you"?

"I want to know where that confidence comes from, so I'm willing to accept you as my student."

What? After that Fauré massacre? I looked at him in astonishment.

"I think music means a lot to you. Let's try to find ways to express it as best as you can."

"Really? You will take me as your student?"

"Yes, but under certain conditions."

"I will take all conditions."

He laughed.

"Listen. First, you will only do a specific series of exercises for the next year, with almost no learning of music involved. Second, you will need to dedicate at least two hours a day to doing those exercises. If you do not have a piano with you on certain days, you will need to practice on a solid surface or a dummy keyboard. Third, you will only register for your exam again, if you wish to, two years from now. And you will pass it. OK?"

"OK."

"So, I'd see you next week at the same time. You do not need to prepare anything. Just bring your Hanon with you."

***

The next year was not easy. In the first few weeks, I did exercises to strengthen the independence of my fingers, build up some strength in my fingertips, and increase my flexibility. I remember taking 30 minutes just to go through the first Hanon exercise at a painstakingly slow tempo, making sure that my fingers were aligned and that no finger was raised when another was playing. We did the exercises with all sorts of different rhythmic and dynamic permutations, working through each of them in different keys. I was refreshed and determined in the first few weeks, but by the third month, I felt so frustrated and exhausted that I would slump my head on the keys halfway through the practice, the clash of sounds understandably causing some confusion for my parents seated in the living room outside. However, I did manage to play some Bach after the first year, and my hand span had increased by a tone.

It was especially difficult because I had almost negligible foundation in my technique. My parents gave in to my requests for piano lessons at the age of 8, after my late uncle gifted my sister and me a toy piano, which revealed to me an expanse I had never experienced. The toy piano was my world. But we fast expended most of our nursery rhymes on the 15-key keyboard, possibly to the dismay of my mother, and started asking for piano classes.

I sped through the classes; there was no stopping me. Very rapidly, we also acquired an upright piano — which was quite an investment for our family at that time — over which my sister and I battled every morning to practice before going to school. The problem was that my technical development could not catch up with my enthusiasm and natural affinity for the piano. For the initial grades, my teachers could find ways to cover up my technical weaknesses very easily, enabling me to ace all exams with little effort. But by the fifth grade, I had to submerge most of my pieces with the pedal to avoid revealing defects.

At this point, I was 13 and I felt that there was no piece in the world that I could not learn myself. I announced to my parents one day that I would embark on a self-taught program, taking the Grade 8 exam myself in two years. During this time, I explored all the repertoire I'd long wanted to play, spending long hours at the piano — at one point I foolishly worked through the Liszt Sonata, studying the music every day wherever I went — but ultimately developing poor habits and eradicating any remnant of technique that was left in me. I did quite well for the exam, but thereafter, I knew I had to seek professional guidance to go further with my diploma examinations.

So, when I went to Prof Yu, there was truly no technique to speak of that remained in my hands. There was no way I could play Bach or Mozart. My fingers were flat, and they generally collapsed. I knew only how to move fast, and to play loud — two characteristics that Prof Yu would have to constantly reign in for the years to come.

***

To this day, I sometimes wonder why Prof Yu had decided to take me in. When we first met, he had returned to Singapore for almost ten years after having been a Professor of Piano at the Royal College of Music (RCM), London for three decades, during which he had also been bestowed the prestigious Fellow of RCM in the same year as Andrew Lloyd Webber. Following his return, he was Vice-Principal of the Nanyang Academy of Fine Arts (NAFA) and started the School of Young Talents. He had an incredulous schedule. On top of his teaching at NAFA and at home, he would sometimes travel to China to discover new talents, or have visitors flying in to have a couple of classes before flying off again. He is also a fantastic bridge player — "I have almost as many bridge books as I have music books," he recently quipped — and can be found playing the game at least thrice a week at the clubs. And these usually take place after his gym sessions.

It was only during the interviewing process for this book that I realized that my dear teacher is already 83 years old today; he certainly was not in his early 60s when I first met him. So why would he take in a terrible student, nowhere near the level of his students past and present, even offering free lessons if I could not afford it, when he probably ought to have been enjoying his retirement?

The process of writing this book has given me a few answers. First, there is no retirement for Prof Yu. During interviews, I have seen his eyes glisten with excitement talking about his upcoming appointments, new students, future collaborations, bridge tournaments, travel plans ("just to take a short break"), and ideas for more books. Our interview sessions were usually squeezed in between a lesson in the morning and lunch in the afternoon — a meal of such simple dishes as steamed fish, braised tofu, and carrot soup with rice, which I heartily devoured. Following that, he usually had to leave for other engagements, while I lugged yet another stack of books home from his library for further research.

Second, Prof Yu believes firmly in helping serious, interested, and industrious students realize their full potential. Over the past months, I have heard him talk about so many different kinds of students past and present, some of whom have become concert pianists, and others, like myself, who simply continue playing the piano as a pastime. When I had the chance to interact with these students, we would have a good laugh about the various disastrous renditions of music we'd delivered in his studio, which were usually met with a typical remark from our teacher as, "Well, I don't think we can play Bach quite like that." But we also realized that the ways in which Prof Yu proceeded to help each of us find our own versions of the music were different: with me he tended to draw connections to literature, with another student who was a major in conducting, he encouraged him to link his experiences at the piano and on the podium. This meant that the same piece could end up sounding vastly different among ourselves — a realization that strikes me very strongly each time I hear another student of his perform. This dedication to teaching, with such care paid to individual personality, strengths, and aptitude, is a quality I try to emulate in my own teaching.

And lastly, Prof Yu enjoys sharing the joy and wonder of music. The pure jubilation in him when he recounted his experiences of listening and playing the Chopin mazurkas (which you will read in Chapter 3) completely bowled me over; he was not recounting, he was truly experiencing it again at that moment, sitting in front of me. He brought me back to London in the 50s, when he, barely in his 20s, was sitting in front of the record player, listening to Arthur Rubinstein in disbelief. Now it was me listening to him in disbelief; I could hear the music, that music from the record player, as he described it. Music moves people; it moves people closer to each other.

***

This book project arose out of the three above-mentioned points: his love for life, education, and music. We had the idea for it quite early in 2012, right after I had given a recital at the Arts House in Singapore to a small audience of 80 — yet another of my stubborn projects which Prof Yu had steadfastly supported ("but only if you practice seven hours a day unwaveringly for the next four months coupled with swimming thrice a week; and drop Schumann's Fantasy please" — I lost 5 kg).

After the recital, I went by Prof Yu's house for tea and some general concluding remarks.

"How do you feel about the recital?" he asked.

"I'm glad I pulled through. But I was dead frightened, especially of having a memory lapse. I'm sorry the Schubert was butchered." (I had made a wrong leap toward the end of the first movement of the D. 784, moving from page 8 to page 2 of the score. I then improvised and leapt back to page 9 after a few bars.)

"You don't have to be sorry. I had no doubt you would pull through. I'm glad you did it."

"Thank you for helping me fulfill this dream."

A sip of tea.

"You leave for England next week, am I right?"

"Yes."

"When do you come home?"

"In December."

"Drop by again. You can play some music and we can discuss a book project, if you're interested."

"Oh?"

"I've been meaning to share some ideas about music and how it relates to life. A sort of short, succinct guide to enjoying classical music for all music-lovers, which at the same time, reveals some insights into the profession that would benefit music students, teachers, and professionals. And I think you might be a suitable writer for that."

"I would love to do it, Prof Yu."

"But on one condition."

"I accept all conditions."

He laughed.

"You're a wild horse. The condition is that you must finish your PhD. We only start writing after you are done with Cambridge."

***

It has been two years since I graduated, and over the course of 14 months, I've returned to Singapore thrice to interview Prof Yu for this book. After close to 50 hours of interviews and lively discussions, I started putting the book together, making sure to keep to Prof Yu's overarching aim of introducing the joy and intricacies of classical piano music to the music-lover at large.

Having said that, I have also put in pockets of detailed musical analysis and historical segments that would interest music students and professionals. The mazurka analysis in Chapter 3, for instance, might prove a little too detailed to a general reader's liking, but it is hoped that such portions of the book will reveal an initial impression of the myriad thought processes that go into musical interpretation and performance.

In addition, I have compiled a listening list (together with a corresponding Spotify playlist) that details the music cited. Such supplementary material would hopefully enhance your reading process, allowing you to relate the words to the sound, the score, and the musical world past and present.

Lastly, I hope that I have managed to convey a sense of the wondrous world of classical music to you, the way Prof Yu has allowed me to experience through my interactions with him, and which he has empowered me to express through my newfound strong(er) fingers. Perhaps, the message he gave to me ten years ago is the same that underpins this book: keep learning, learn seriously, and spread the joy. I hope that this is the energy that such a short introduction to classical music leaves you with.

Part 1

Where to Place the Grace Note?

Chapter 1

No Time Given to the Flourish

1.1 Why Grace Notes?

LL: I hope to discuss with you an aspect of classical piano music
that I have always struggled with — grace notes.[1] These additional notes are meant to decorate the main line, but trying to
fit them in smoothly is a perpetual challenge since it's never
clear where precisely they should be placed, or how they should
be executed (Figure 1).

CY: Start with the positive: instead of concentrating too much on
trying to fit them in, think about how you can make use of them
to enhance the line and henceforth to crystallize the character
of the music in your own way.

Figure 1:   Excerpt from the first movement of Mozart's Piano Sonata in C Major,
K. 279, showing frequent use of grace notes (in small print) in the melodic line.

---

[1]We begin our discussion of grace notes from its traditional definition as small
notation (appoggiatura and acciaccatura) but extend its implications to other
kinds of ornamentation, such as signs (mordents, trills, turns, etc.).

LL: In what ways do grace notes enhance the line?

CY: Grace notes stem from our desire to embellish and beautify things, especially if they would otherwise seem bare, mundane, or repetitive. When we have notes that are held for a long time, the addition of grace notes can enhance — or in the case of the harpsichord, sustain — the single sound with added texture, shape, or purpose. In some cases, they can even announce the arrival of the main note.

LL: You mean grace notes can enhance the melody by way of anticipation?

CY: Yes. In fact, a simple example might help here.

At one point in the twentieth century it became so fashionable to play both hands slightly out of sync to the extent that notes written together were almost never sounded together. Sometimes the right hand entered a fraction of a second later than the left, and vice versa. When overused it became a mannerism, but when used strategically — and we still occasionally hear it today — it can be quite attractive. Where does its merit lie?

Imagine that you first hear a low bass note and then a split second later a high note is sounded — the melodic note makes an entrance! The high note draws out the juice of the harmony . . . yet, at the same time, it appears to land on a bass cushion that supports it. Or consider the reverse. You hear the melodic note, and nothing below . . . there's a fraction of tension here — Who's going to support the main character? This anticipation of the harmony enhances the melodic line and makes the listener more acutely aware of surprising harmonic resonances.

Grace notes sometimes work in the same way. They enhance the principal note by making us wait for it, the same way important people tend to have a desire to appear slightly late . . .

Figure 2:   Excerpt from the first movement of Mozart's Piano Sonata in C Major, K. 279.

LL: So, in this sense, grace notes enhance the melodic line by punctuating it, or almost spot-lighting it.

CY: Yes, and very often, the ways in which grace notes uplift the melody or add flavor to certain notes can result in very different impressions of the same melodic line.

Take this excerpt of Mozart's First Piano Sonata. How would you play the grace notes in the fourth bar? (Figure 2)

LL: Given that the movement is rather fast and its overall character light, playful, and full of contrasts, I would play these grace notes rather rapidly, almost simultaneously with the main notes, creating an airy impression with some bounce to it.

CY: That is a possibility. But also consider another interpretation: Can we not execute each grace note with a little lilt (slightly stress the grace note and lift off on the main note) — DE-um DE-um DE-um DE-um, and so on — making the whole line sound graceful? In your interpretation we have a line that is spirited and carefree; in the second it becomes slightly more thoughtful and elegant. Both are legitimate and attractive; it is up to the performer to find out what he or she wants to say with the grace note.

LL: So, there is no fixed way to execute grace notes even within a specific bar of music?

CY: Grace notes are quite imaginary — they are not really there. They are often suggestions that bring the pianist out of the score. In that sense, they are flexible and allow the pianist a certain degree of freedom in expression.

1.2 Grace Within Limits

LL: What you've just said about freedom is surprising given the prescriptive way students tend to be taught grace notes or ornaments at a young age: appoggiaturas on the beat, or trills always starting on the note above for Bach. How do we balance this regimented way of learning with the more flexible nature of the grace note that you've mentioned?

CY: Here we're approaching a more fundamental question concerning training.

A single grace note always appears within a larger context. What function is it serving in relation to the line and the harmony? Which musical period does the piece belong to? Who is the composer? In which style is the piece composed? Some background knowledge will allow the pianist to identify and consider the overarching boundaries that the single grace note is set in. For example, one must be aware that there are composers who gave rather specific guidelines for ornamentation in their own music such as C. P. E. Bach and Couperin.

Good training enables the pianist to consider — rather than be bound by — these larger contexts in interpreting grace notes. A basic understanding of Bach's keyboard music will reveal that his conception and notation of grace notes changed throughout his life; strictly following his ornament table (written as a teaching aid for his young son then) for *all* his pieces would be too simplistic. And given that notation for grace notes can vary within a composer's lifetime, it should come as no surprise that it differed between composers of the same musical period or country.

LL: So, the "regimented way" of learning grace notes ought to be more open and flexible in the first place?

CY: Yes, and even then, knowing more and discovering new avenues in your learning process is not enough. You must consider all legitimate guidelines and find a version that resonates with you.

LL: What does that mean?

CY: Gather as many resources as possible and find out what suits your personality and style best. All performers are different — something that works for another performer might not feel natural to you. While music is most frequently seen as a form of artistic expression, it is also a fantastic resource for discovering yourself.

LL: Does listening to recordings of music help in this regard?

CY: Yes, but it's crucial to first study the score yourself, formulate an informed understanding of the music, then gather some personal response to the music by listening to others. Take for example — well, why don't you tell me a piece you are working on?

LL: At the moment, I'm looking at Bach's "Goldberg Variations".

CY: And are you inspired by any recording or performance of it?

LL: I was very much moved by Igor Levit's performance in Cambridge some two years ago. But prior to that, I was greatly inspired by Glenn Gould's renditions.

CY: Tell me what you liked about them.

LL: I found Levit's execution smooth yet highly personal. His treatment of the 25th variation was painstakingly slow with every note impeccably placed, yet one never lost the direction of the overarching lines. He was able to convey his love for the music to the audience, as if he were discovering all those beautiful turns and falling intervals for the first time.

With Gould, I remain captivated by the differences and similarities in his two renditions made 26 years apart. His mathematical precision with ornaments persists despite the vast differences in speed! To me, there's something very organic yet mortal about listening to the two Goulds . . .

CY: There's indeed much to be appreciated from Gould's very different treatments of the same piece. Performers do change with time, and oftentimes our interpretations grow with us.

But the reason for my question is to give you some ideas on how you can expand your listening perspective. If you're captivated by the contrasts in Gould's recordings, why not explore András Schiff's two Goldberg recordings a generation later? When you listen to Schiff for the first time after being used to Gould, you might be struck by how brisk and buoyant the Goldberg can sound! Appreciate this general impression on first listening, and then listen closely the second time for detailed transformations in his recordings. You speak of being captivated by the same exactness of ornaments in Gould, but perhaps you can be similarly inspired by how Schiff uses them differently in both recordings to convey a sense of flexibility and improvisation.

And if you appreciate Levit's more personal, romantic interpretation, why not listen to someone completely different, like Landowska? Her Pleyel harpsichord might sound initially heavy to ears used to the modern piano but be patient and you'd uncover a different kind of romanticism — a grand manner of execution that veers toward the epic. Is there something we can learn from her way of playing the harpsichord for the modern piano today?

So, learn to listen with a purpose. On first listening, try to forget about the score. Draw the flavor out of the playing, completely immerse yourself in the music, and be inspired by each pianist's strengths. On second hearing, focus on the details — listen to every single turn and nuance. Dig deeper into each interpretation and use it to increase your understanding of the score.

When broadening your listening repertoire, first know the aspects that attract you, and then find out how other recordings enhance or shed light on these aspects. This will help you gather a stronger personal response to the piece. But perhaps most importantly: don't be governed by what you hear, and most certainly don't copy.

LL: It's interesting you mention Landowska in this context — didn't she once say to Pablo Casals, "You play Bach your way and I play him his way"?

CY: That's an interesting anecdote because it concerns the execution of Bach's trills. Reportedly, Landowska jokingly said those words to Casals after he had told her he was unconvinced of why she always started her trills from the note above.[2]

---

[2]According to Landowska's pupil and confidante Denise Restout, her words to Casals were "Mon cher Pau, ne discutons pas davantage. Continuez a jouer Bach a votre façon et moi, a sa façon." (My dear Pau, let's not argue further. Continue playing Bach your way and I, his way.) Landowska reportedly offered the original edition of Leopold Mozart's *Violinschule* (1756) as further evidence of starting trills from the note above. Refer to the online music digest HPSCHD-L (September, 1996).

She was quite a character with strong convictions. Yet interestingly, if you listen closely to her Goldberg, you'd realize that her trills may always start from the note above, but they all serve different functions. There are moments when they are executed like a tremendous flourish, sounding very free and expressive indeed.

No symbol can adequately capture everything we feel. Trills can be steady and precise, or romantic, even improvisatory. Musicians have to go beyond the score to begin understanding what the music can bring. And grace notes offer us an excellent opportunity for that.

1.3 Grace Notes: Good to Have or Must Have?

LL: Taking just the recordings we've mentioned as examples, I'm struck by how flexibly grace notes can be executed. Performers frequently deviate from the grace notes indicated, and quite often the same grace notes are played differently when repeated! Is this common practice? How strictly should we follow the indications on the score?

CY: To answer your question, one has to go back to the root of grace notes: improvisation.

Musical ornamentation was very much central to Baroque music. For Italian opera singers of the seventeenth and eighteenth centuries, embellishment was a must-have, essentially on a par with the voice; how well a singer could improvise a given line was an indication of skill and virtuosity. In fact, some composers left their score unadorned, so singers could extemporize according to their own abilities.

However, this led to a problem: excessiveness. C. P. E. Bach wrote humorously that unrestrained use of ornamentation was akin to spices destroying the perfect dish.[3] Imagine if every musician in a chamber group or orchestra improvised — no one would be able to hear anything. Complete freedom is complete chaos . . .

Hence, this excessiveness became one main reason why notation using grace notes and symbols came into the picture: it allowed composers to temper the use of ornamentation and regain some control over how their music actually sounded. While some composers adopted such notation to reflect a precise execution of their music, others used them as approximations to give performers some basic, regulatory suggestions.

LL: Does this mean that grace notes can offer the classical pianist today moments of improvisation?

CY: It doesn't quite work like that. It's more important for the pianist to find out what function the grace note is performing in that specific musical context, rather than to cut to the chase and treat every grace note as an opportunity to improvise.

The whole story of how grace note notation came into being is highly complex. On the one hand, it helped to reduce excessive ornamentation as previously mentioned. Yet on the other hand, those were sometimes moments that the composer left open for themselves in the process of composition. Composers can change their minds about their works, you know. Some Baroque masters would be quite surprised to see us poring over the precise execution of a specific grace note today.

Also, don't forget that the masters themselves were superb improvisers: one cannot imagine Bach, Mozart, Beethoven,

---

[3] See C. P. E. Bach, *Essay on the True Art of Playing Keyboard Instruments* (London: W. W. Norton, 1985), trans. and ed. by William J. Mitchell, p. 81.

or Liszt not improvising. For instance, there's an amusing account of Beethoven's improvisatory prowess recorded by his student Reis: when challenged to an improvisation duel by German virtuoso Daniel Steibelt, Beethoven apparently took a page of Steibelt's composition, turned it upside down, and improvised a theme from the first few measures with just one finger.[4]

LL: It's fascinating to learn about how improvisation was very much a part of classical music some 200–300 years ago. Is it fair to say that it has died down in classical music today, though not in jazz?

CY: Classical pianists today do offer some brief moments of improvisation in their interpretations, but improvisation during the Baroque times was of quite a different nature: it was integral to both composition and performance. Keyboardists had to routinely play improvised accompaniment from figured bass, for instance (Figures 3 and 4). And cadenzas were generally not written out for the soloists until Beethoven.[5]

Suffice it to say that a trained keyboardist of those times was expected to have some grounding in the different aspects of improvisation — not just harmonic (i.e., to improvise upon

---

[4]See Thayer et al. (eds.), *Thayer's Life of Beethoven*, Vol. 1 (New Jersey: Princeton University Press, 1991), p. 257.

[5]Cadenzas were typically virtuosic, improvised passages played by the soloist toward the end of a concerto movement. The orchestra remains silent while the soloist performs, typically reprising thematic material of the work and often-times without strict meter. Interestingly (and somewhat ironically), the soloist often signals the end of the cadenza with a grace — a trill, or even a ladder of trills — whereupon the orchestra rejoins on a strong cadence ("cadence" being the root word of "cadenza"). By his Fifth Piano Concerto, Beethoven explicitly wrote in his score, "Non si fa una Cadenza, ma s'attacca subito il seguente (Do not play a cadenza, but instead proceed immediately to the following)," whereupon a fully written-out 20-bar cadenza was presented.

Figure 3: Original manuscript of the opening bars of Bach's Double Violin Concerto in D Minor, BWV 1043. The last stave, with "Basso" indicated in the left margin, shows the music ("figured bass") for the basso continuo, with the small numbers above the written bass line indicating the harmony to be realized by the accompanist. Figure 4 will show how the "Basso," for which Bach has only written a single line (the left hand), can be played in full with both hands due to the chords indicated by small numbers.

Figure 4: An example of how the harpsichord would sound with the figured bass realized. Notice that the left hand plays the music indicated by Bach, but the right hand is made up by the harpsichordist with reference to the figured bass. The boxed notes in Figure 3, which were indicated with the numbers 6 above them, now have the indicated chords realized in the right hand: the number "6" was short for "6/3," meaning that notes sixth and third from the bass note had to be realized to form a first-inversion chord. Note that this is just one version of the many that can be realized from the figured bass of the basso continuo.

a certain harmonic progression), but also thematic, melodic, formal, and so on. Bach was known to improvise for hours uninterrupted on a single subject; the "Goldberg Variations", apparently written to ease Count Kaiserling's insomnia, provide an exposition of this. Hence, executing improvisatory embellishments of the melodic line — partly approximated as grace notes on the score — would be barely scraping the surface.

LL: So why are classical pianists today not expected to have the same grounding in improvisation?

CY: Partly because we now have access to a tremendous amount of repertoire — no one can finish exploring this in a lifetime, still less to master the art of good improvisation.

Another reason would be the separation between the composer and performer. Remember that the best improvisers then were frequently the composers themselves who were also performers of their own pieces. Today, performers are more generally seen as interpreters of others' compositions. Because of this power or authority shift, we start asking questions like: What was the original intention of the composer? How can we give as authentic a representation of the composition as possible? Hence the *urtext*[6] craze has, to some extent, become the order of the day, and its restrictive nature is rather at odds with the free spirit of improvisation.

What I've given you is an extremely condensed and simplified account of how grace notes evolved from being a must-have to

---

[6]An *urtext* edition aims primarily to provide an authentic, original version of the music as intended by the composer. This not only means reproducing the composer's facsimile, but also comparing it to the composer's revisions and previous published editions, as well as combining it with research from music historians and theorists. This can be differentiated from a performance edition, in which elements such as simplified notation, phrase markings, and expressive indications have been added by the editor.

a good-to-have in classical piano music. And it's a completely different course of history from, say jazz, or Chinese classical music. In the latter, there remains a pure proliferation of grace notes and other kinds of ornamentation; one can say that the technique *is* grace note.

1.4 Where to Place the Grace Note?

LL: This is all very fascinating, but it still doesn't help the clueless student deal with the practicalities of the grace note. They are a real nuisance to fit in . . . the greater the number of notes, the bigger the headache! I remember my early grade teachers used to strike them out with the pencil when I first learnt a piece, only to hastily squeeze them back in as late as the week before I had to play the piece for an exam. Since then, I've always found them a bit of an irritating accessory.

CY: The clueless student obviously needs a teacher! Grace notes can be a problem because they are not, strictly speaking, given time in the music. Yet they take time to execute — they need time. This means that they must borrow the time from somewhere. But how and where exactly?

To find the answer, first omit the grace note. Remember, a grace note should serve the purpose of enhancing something. This means that it should never be squeezed into the music — it needs air. Second, grace notes should not interfere: they can add tension or uncertainty to the music, but they should not confuse, still less rock, the harmonic foundation of the music. And the same with rhythm: they should neither diffuse nor encroach on the rhythmic flow of the music.

With these in mind, you can then make contextual decisions about the timing of the grace notes. For instance, grace notes can sometimes serve the function of connecting notes. So, ask yourself: Is the grace note leading on from the previous note or onto the next note? This will help you decide whether to borrow time from the note preceding or following the grace note.

LL: In other words, there are at once too few and too many guidelines on how exactly to place grace notes.

CY: Grace notes strive on freedom. But the freedom falls within certain regulations and guidelines, much as life itself. To know how to fully appreciate and utilize them, you need to first learn to be bound to much training, listening, studying, and understanding. Starting with the most basic units of music could help in this respect.

Chapter 2

A Phrase By Any Other Name

2.1 Hunting Phrases

LL: You mentioned that returning to the most basic units of music could help to increase my understanding of grace notes. In this respect, perhaps we could start with phrases. I understand that a phrase is made up of numerous aspects: shape, rhythm, harmony, interval, and so on. With all these in hand, how can we begin to understand what a phrase is?

CY: Knowing the different components of a phrase is different from knowing what it is, and even further from knowing how to interpret it — phrasing is arguably the most desired refinement and the greatest charm in performance.

Now, let me flip the question back to you. In your years of teaching music to young children, how have you taught them to understand the concept of a music phrase?

LL: It's always been tough, but I found that very young children understand it quite well if I explain by way of recourse to language. So, in the midst of a lesson, I would suddenly start talking without pauses and breaks in my sentences, which undoubtedly cracks up the young ones. I then explain to them that just as a spoken story needs small pauses between and

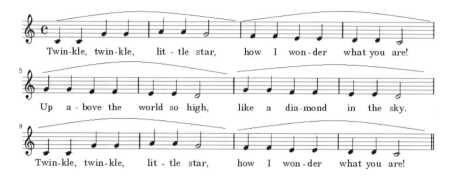

Figure 1:   The most commonly sung verse of "Twinkle Twinkle Little Star".
Each curved line demarcates a single phrase.

within sentences for us to make sense of the words, so too a song needs phrases for us to make sense of the notes.

Then as a little activity, I have them sing "Twinkle Twinkle Little Star" in a single breath without pauses (invariably leading to great pandemonium), and then on the second attempt, to sing with little pauses at their discretion. They intuitively take a breath after every phrase without any prior knowledge of phrasing — that makes it very convenient for me to explain to them what a phrase is (Figure 1).

CY: By linking phrasing to speech and breathing, you're tapping on the essence and *naturalness* of a phrase. You've given them the impression that: first, a phrase is made up of a series of notes — a single note cannot be a phrase; second, a phrase generally has a discernible start and end; and third, phrases of the same song tend to have equal lengths and share some similarities.

In all, it's probably a reasonable start.

LL: Going on from there is not always easy though. After all, it's one thing to take a breath when singing phrases, and another to translate this to piano playing. The picture gets even cloudier when we consider music phrases that are not necessarily tunes

Figure 2:   Manuscript of Chopin's Nocturne in G Minor, op. 37 no. 1. Curved lines stretched above a group of notes indicate that they form a phrase.

or melodies that you can sing — here the analogy to speech and breathing becomes more tenuous.

CY: One step at a time. Let's first take a more detailed look at identifying phrases in the context of classical piano pieces. Sometimes, composers will help us with indications in the score, as in this Chopin nocturne for instance (Figure 2).

Chopin has very clearly indicated the phrasing in both hands. In particular, note that the left hand has an extremely long phrase in the third line that actually stretches into the first beat of the next line; this long phrase happens at the same time as the shorter phrases in the right hand, thus creating an interesting musical texture.

But even when composers don't indicate the phrasing, the performer should be able to find them. In the earlier example, what are some hints in the music that would help you to phrase the notes in the right hand, if phrase signs were not indicated?

Figure 3:   First 8 bars of Chopin's Nocturne in G Minor, op. 37 with rests circled.

Figure 4:   First 2 bars of Chopin's Nocturne in G Minor, op. 37 with the rest and long note circled.

LL: Taking just the first two lines, I'd say that the rests play a very important role. They seem to indicate moments analogous to a speaker or a singer pausing to take a breath before restarting (Figure 3).

So, if I were to take the first phrase as lasting till the first rest — meaning that the phrase is only four beats long — I would be inclined to see if it makes any musical sense for the second phrase to be of this length too. And in some respects, it does. Instead of a rest, we would have a long note at the end of the second phrase, somewhat responding with more gravity to the rest that curtailed the first phrase with uncertainty (Figure 4).

The third phrase that follows from these two phrases then seems rather natural to me. Where both the first two phrases consisted of falling notes, the third phrase seems to tell us that all hope is not lost: it picks up the low note and starts to pull it up with climbing notes . . . but will it last? (Figure 5)

Figure 5:   Chopin's Nocturne in G Minor, op. 37 with some characteristics of the first four phrases highlighted.

Alas! The third phrase ends with a fall into a long, low note again, and we're not sure where we are headed after this . . . but enter the fourth phrase, which heroically resuscitates the drop with a dramatic leap in sound — optimism is affirmed. Yet, this optimism is again quickly undercut with the decrescendo . . .

CY: Thank you, what an eventful journey right from the outset!

You speak of the third phrase sounding natural to you after two consecutive falling phrases; isn't that naturalness also an effect of the reassuring and resounding "G" in both hands (first note of both hands in bar 3), clearly reinstating the key and giving us an impression of returning home briefly after the slight unease of the first two phrases? This brief sense of security is further enhanced by the brief passage through the relative major in bar 4, finally culminating in the last note "D" of the fourth right-hand phrase, which is also shared by the first note of the fifth phrase.

The interaction between a line's contour and its harmony can introduce moments of tension and relief, thereby giving the pianist some clues on where the phrases lie. But knowing how to play them is another story. The same phrase when approached as a positive statement would sound completely different when approached with uncertainty.

LL: So just as intonation can drastically change the meaning of the same sentence, the way a phrase is played can result in very different impressions of the same series of notes?

CY: Chopin had a reputation of seldom playing the same phrase twice alike. He was said to have varied his expressions of the same piece or even the same line depending on such factors as the venue or his mood at that moment. In fact, there's an interesting account of this given by one of his students, Henri Péru. After a certain class where Chopin personally demonstrated how a piece should be played, Péru returned the next lesson and played the piece confidently convinced that he had masterfully mimicked Chopin's rendition. Unexpectedly, Chopin rose from his couch disapprovingly and again demonstrated how it ought to be played. Péru was left utterly dejected — the new rendition was completely different from the previous.[1]

Clearly, Chopin could have done that deliberately to serve a pedagogical purpose, but the point is well taken: the notes may be the same, but the ways to phrase them are infinite.

LL: How, then, do we move from identifying phrases to knowing how to play them?

CY: To answer this, let's go back to where we started: the naturalness of a phrase. When in doubt, ask this simple question: How would a singer sing this phrase?

2.2 Singing Phrases

LL: I have always thought that singing only helped my young students in their first phrasing class with "Twinkle Twinkle Little Star." How does singing help in developing our understanding of phrasing?

---

[1] See Jean-Jacques Eigeldinger, *Chopin: Pianist and Teacher* (Cambridge: Cambridge University Press, 1988), p. 55.

CY: Did you know that when Daniel Barenboim had doubts about a phrase, he would ask Jacqueline Du Pré to sing it for him? When Jacqueline was too ill to play the cello, she continued to teach by singing the music. She was fascinated by the relation between notes: a single note or chord by itself is lifeless, she said, but when next to another it "immediately speaks, has countour, geographical significance, and expression." And even when this interval between the two notes was as minute as a minor second, she could make it the most expressive slide, traversing the greatest emotional distance.[2]

In singing, some key musical elements are brought to our attention. What kind of shape do we have here? Where is the phrase going? Where are the moments of tension and relaxation? Are there rhythmic characteristics that shine through? A quick example might help here. Say we look at march phrases. Why don't you sing me a march phrase?

LL: The first march phrase that comes to my mind — and this is not indicative of my feelings toward our conversation — is Chopin's *Funeral March* (Figure 6).

MARCHE FUNÈBRE.

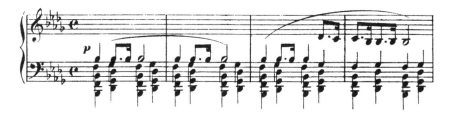

Figure 6:   First two phrases of Chopin's funeral march from the third movement of his Piano Sonata No. 2 in B-flat Minor, op. 37.

[2] See Elizabeth Wilson, *Jacqueline Du Pré, Her Life, Her Music, Her Legend* (New York: Faber & Faber, 1999), p. 421.

BAM--BAM-Be-BAM-------- ... (*singing continues*)

CY: Now contrast this phrase with the nocturne that we discussed previously. Are different musical elements highlighted here?

LL: Where the shape and direction of the phrase seemed to take center stage in the nocturne, here it's the rhythmic momentum that drives the march phrase. The dotted rhythm in the right hand stoically chugs the phrase forward while the steady chords in the left hand seem to anchor the phrase into an undertone of sombre dread.

CY: Fair observations. Now try singing the funeral march phrase with a different sound. Imagine you are a xylophone.

LL: Ding--ding-ding-ding------- ... This doesn't really work.

CY: What does this show us? In addition to contour and harmony, function can sometimes be central to a phrase. In other words, ask yourself: What does the phrase do? When you have a march phrase, it conveys a certain momentum, articulation, atmosphere. A march phrase can be soft, as Chopin has indicated, but it should never be weak. In the rare instance that a march phrase creeps in, we should imagine hearing it from a distance — faintly pronounced rather than weakly articulated.

And this is why you had imagined this march phrase as having a certain kind of timbre and register to match its function. You immediately articulated the notes with "BAM" rather than "ding," or "la" for that matter — perhaps with the sound of a brass instrument at the back of your mind. So it may appear surprising, but instrumentation can sometimes help a pianist with phrasing too.

LL: Yet it seems to me that not all phrases can be conceived of with different instrumentation or straightforwardly singable lines. Much of Liszt's or Chopin's music seems to be highly pianistic. Chopin's impromptus, for instance, seem to begin with a similar musical texture or effect, much like a twirl of sound that escapes. But that's not the kind of phrase that we'd characterize as singable or to be played by any instrument other than the piano.

CY: And yet Chopin sent his students to the opera house to learn phrasing! *Il faut chanter avec les doigts*, he reminded his students, *you must sing with the fingers*. And interestingly, he regarded the pianist's wrist as the "respiration in the voice" — the wrist should rise and fall with great suppleness to correspond to a singer's breathing.[3]

Now, bear in mind that the elements of a phrase are various and its possibilities endless; timbre, register, and instrumentation are some ingredients that can help the pianist to phrase imaginatively, just as contour, harmony, rhythm, and function also play a part. So, instead of applying this whole host of ingredients to all phrases, set out trying to discover the multitude of ingredients in any single phrase within a specific context — at every turn you will find so many angles, so many surprises.

2.3 Phrases of Foreign Lands

2.3.1 *Overcoming the shortcomings of an instrument*

LL: Now that you have given me an introduction to some basic elements of phrasing, I wonder if we could look at three specific phrasing problems that I'm struggling with.

CY: Shoot off.

LL: The first is rather embarrassing. It concerns sustaining long singing phrases on the piano. The piece I'm thinking about here is Chopin's Prelude in E Minor (Figure 7).

---

[3] See Eigeldinger, p. 44.

Figure 7:   First 8 bars of Chopin's Prelude in E Minor, op. 28 no. 4. The long singing phrases of the melody in the right hand are highlighted. Notice that the accompanying left hand is made up of steady, changing chords.

Despite having such simple notes — it's probably one of the first Chopin pieces that students touch — and an instantly memorable or recognizable tune (it might be the most quoted Chopin piece outside classical music, think Radiohead, Serge Gainsbourg, Tom Jobim . . .), I struggle to this day trying to sustain the long phrases in the right hand.

CY: Be more specific about your problem. What exactly about sustaining them do you struggle with?

LL: I guess there are two aspects to this problem. First, I find it difficult to sustain the length of the notes. While I can imagine a singer singing the melody as an unbroken line, I find that my line on the piano keeps dipping and breaking due to the natural fading away of the notes — a mechanical restriction or shortcoming of the instrument.

Second, I find it very difficult to make these long phrases interesting to the listener because there is not much happening. Unlike the Chopin nocturne and march that we've briefly looked at, this melody has very little going for it insofar as contour, rhythm, and function are concerned. With long, repeated notes mainly going down in steps, it's as if I had to captivate the listener with a story about a man strolling in the rain.

CY: And yet you like the piece.

LL: I've adored this piece since I was a child.

CY: What do you like about it?

LL: I've liked it for different reasons. When I was younger, I simply found it very moving without knowing why. When I started to understand it more, I grew fascinated by how the harmonic changes in the creeping chords of the left hand could create such emotional depth beneath a bare, simple melody.

CY: I think you've found the answer for yourself. Instead of asking how you can sustain the line in the right hand, why not ask: How can I shape the chords in the left hand to create the *illusion* of the phrase in the right hand continuing? A large part of the beauty in this piece lies in the underpinning chords — each change of the chord imparts a different flavor to the melody and steers it in a different direction.

So how does this translate to actual playing? When you are playing those chords in the left hand, ask yourself: Where is this chord moving next? Which part of the chord is changing? Can I direct the listener's attention to a subtle change or a certain movement between chords which might otherwise go unnoticed?

Use this undercurrent in the left hand to move the long phrases in your right hand. The question, then, is not so much how to sustain a long note — there's little we can do about the inevitability of long notes fading away on the piano — but rather, how do I play the next note? What happened in the left hand before that? Or even, what is happening with the left hand at that moment, and beyond?

LL: In other words, the harmonic texture in the left hand actually shapes and sustains the listener's impression of the melody in the right hand?

CY: It's an illusion you are conveying — just because the sound vanishes at points doesn't mean it is not there. When your man goes strolling in the rain, the road might be occluded now and again, but there are so many subtleties and details you can point out along the way that can make the journey interesting.

Say we take a simple example: the opening phrase of Beethoven's "Moonlight Sonata." Similarly, there isn't much contour to speak of, yes? But listen to the movement of those chords (Figure 8).

Now, something interesting happens in the third bar. What can you tell me about that specific chord highlighted?

LL: I think it's a chord that creates tension — there's something unexpected about it. It almost creates an opening in the music and wants to move it toward a stronger chord, perhaps.

CY: Let's be more specific. What kind of chord is this?

Figure 8:   Opening bars of Beethoven's "Moonlight Sonata," op. 27 no. 2, with the discussed chord boxed up.

LL: It's a supertonic chord with a flattened second in the first inversion . . . which makes it the Neapolitan Sixth. Ah, I guess it makes a bit more sense to me now why it sounds so expressive.

CY: Strikes a different chord, literally. Theoretically speaking, certain chords impart a certain flavor and have an expressive function — they become integral to phrasing. The Neapolitan Sixth is an effective chord especially for modulations and cadences. And it is not an archaic classical feature — it's used in music everywhere, including the Beatles[4] . . . .

LL: Is that so? I enjoy the Beatles tremendously, but I have never thought of their music in this light.

CY: In fact, I went to a Beatles concert when I was in London in the 60s. It was the talk of town, so I had to find out for myself what it was all about. Now, I walked in through one door — and out the other instantly. There was no Beatles to be heard, just girls screaming!

Suffice it to say, I did not venture into the Beatles for some time after this. But sometimes you must try to keep the door ajar even if your immediate reaction might be a lack of acceptance. Indeed, when I listened to them much later in life, I did find them refreshing and enjoyable — a true product of the time.

2.3.2 *Not taking notation at its face value*

CY: Going back to your narrative about the lone man strolling in the rain, did you know that the Chopin prelude was given the title "Quelles larmes au fond du cloître humide?" ("What tears in the depths of the damp cloister?") by George Sand? Perhaps your narrative could be modified to reflect the cold

---

[4]Take, for instance, the F Major chord that falls on the word "really" in the second line of "Do You Want to Know a Secret." Other examples can be found in Jacques Brel's "Ne Me Quitte Pas" and The Rolling Stones' "Mother's Little Helper," details of which are given in the music cited list.

Figure 9:   Bars 71–74 of Finale alla Fantasia of Schumann's *Variations on the name Abegg*, op. 1.

winter that a very ill Chopin spent writing the preludes in a monastery in Mallorca . . .

LL: How interesting — instrumental music might not refer to actual things in the world the way language does, and yet how vividly it conjures such an atmosphere. And this brings me to my second problem, which concerns phrases that are so imaginative they seem impossible to execute on the piano. Take these few bars in Schumann's *Variations on the name Abegg* (Figure 9).

This phrase appears to be highly imaginative, almost literary to me. Clearly, Schumann is referring us back to the name "Abegg" on which the variations are based, but he is also thoroughly conceptualizing the pianistic sound. The accents (indicated as ">," meaning to give more emphasis) over the last notes cannot be executed: the bass note E and last note G are simply held over from the chord, rather than struck again, so there's no way the pianist can make them louder, given that a held note on the piano simply dies away.

But what can Schumann mean then? Is it a form of symbolic rather than realized notation — to give emphasis by way of withdrawal and absence? Or a kind of abstract imagination of the pianistic sound?

CY: It is all of these — an allusion, illusion, elusion, or even a joke. There are possibilities: (a) omit the phrase (ad lib.) and leave the time void to the imagination of the audience; (b) in an

Figure 10:   Bars 60–64 from the fourth movement of Beethoven's Sonata No. 4 in E-flat Major, op. 7. Note that there is a crescendo between the first and second held octaves in the boxed portion.

intimate surrounding under perfect conditions, play the phrase as written, that is, releasing the notes progressively, the effect can be magical; or (c) play unashamedly the melody direct as indicated by other worthy editions.[5]

In fact, you probably encounter such phrases all the time — though not necessarily in this overtly experimental form — and especially in combination with the first problem you mentioned. The key to playing them is to expand ways of conceiving of them in the first place. Let me give you two simple examples (Figure 10).

What are we to do when Beethoven instructs us to do a crescendo on a held note? It is simply not possible, however hard you insist. It is possible to gradually get louder over a series of notes, but a single note, once struck on the piano, can only get softer.

In this case, the note itself is not the crux — it is what comes after. Inside you, imagine that the sound grows as you hold it (and it may help to think of an instrument that can do this, say the violin), so you have a clear idea of how to place the next note. When conceived of in this manner, this series of octaves hence becomes more dramatic, expressive, and musical.

So again, it's an illusion you are conveying — and even if it takes you a long time to feel this, you must try to cultivate

---

[5] For instance, the Henle Verlag 1977 edition.

Figure 11:   Bars 32–39 from Schubert's *Moments Musicaux*, D. 780 no. 5 in F Minor, with the discussed notes boxed up.

Figure 12:   The pair of notes circled in each hand are written as different notes even though they sound the same on the piano (i.e., G-flat and F-sharp both refer to the same black key on the piano).

> it. Consider this second example from Schubert's *Moments Musicaux*, where once again, we encounter something quite illusive appearing in a different disguise (Figure 11).
>
> Can you tell me quite simply what's peculiar about the notes highlighted?

LL: Some of the notes sound exactly the same even though they are written differently (Figure 12).

CY: And why do you think Schubert wrote these notes enharmonically? After all, he could have just written two G-flats or two F-sharps.

LL: I think writing the notes enharmonically signals a change in sound or a shift in the key to the pianist. So even though the notes sound the same in terms of pitch, they ought to be conceived of and projected differently to convey a shift in character or mood.

CY: Indeed, the difference on the piano may be very subtle since we *must* play the same black key, but other instrumentalists, say the violinist, would register this change immediately and project a rather different sound, perhaps by way of shifts or positions. In fact, in such music systems that use quarter tones as the Arabic, G-flat and F-sharp refer to markedly different pitches.

So Schubert — whose music, by the way, is full of all these enharmonic notes — is not asking the pianist to imagine playing a different note *per se*, but rather, to traverse into a different tonality, a different soundscape.

2.3.3 *Understanding the element of time in music*

CY: But let's take a break from talking about all these illusive things. You mentioned you had a third phrasing problem?

LL: Yes, I do. It concerns phrases whose execution and musical function equally elude me.

CY: What can that possibly mean?

LL: It means I'm at a loss of what to do with those phrases. I don't know what role they serve in relation to the main themes of the music and what musical features to bring out; I don't know why they are there in the music. It's similar to stumbling upon a sentence written in a foreign language.

CY: This does not sound good. Which phrase is it?

LL: It's from Schubert's Sonata in A Minor, D. 784 (Figure 13).

CY: These phrase are, perhaps, best understood as a state of mind.

LL: What do you mean?

CY: Treat them as supposititious interjections that fit into a time frame (three beats) but are unrelated to phrases before or after — a sudden escape from status quo (*sordini* means una

Figure 13: Opening bars of the second movement of Schubert's Sonata in A Minor, D. 784. The phrases in question are boxed up.

Figure 14: Opening bars of Schubert's Sonata in B-flat Major, D. 960. The murmur is boxed up.

corda in Schubert). In this sense, they take up a definite time in playing, but their impact on the music is more of a temporal lapse, an eclipse, an imaginative vacuum — it's almost as if a different narrator to the story has suddenly emerged and vanished. When you think this way, the metamorphoses that follow are pure magic.

Schubert is quite fond of this. Take a look, for instance at his last piano sonata (Figure 14).

Don't you think there's something dark about this murmur? It's emerging from a world completely divorced from what preceded it and time is momentarily frozen. Through these "interruptions," we can sense a strong element of uncertainty. Incidentally, both sonatas were written when Schubert was very ill — you would have noticed that there are many other grim and tragic elements in both sonatas beyond these murmurs.

And that's why when you face phrasing problems of a similar nature in future, it would help to study the composer and his or her works a little more. Remember I said that it's important to discover what the phrase gives you in its context? These Schubert phrases serve as a good example. Rather than straightforwardly applying all those phrasing elements to them, strive to uncover their implications and extensions within their musical and historical contexts. By entering the composer's world, you will gain very valuable input on how to play their music.

2.4 Beyond Phrases

LL: At this point, it seems to me we have come full circle from where we've started. Knowing all the aspects that make up a phrase is good, and probably necessary, but they come to naught when we're faced with highly imaginative or abstract phrases.

CY: That's perplexity, but also beauty — imagine your options, the sheer infinitude of phrasing.

But suppose you remain stuck and frustrated even after using all your resources, why not seek inspiration in other places?

For instance, I've always enjoyed conducting alongside performing the piano. In conducting, the whole orchestra may be working very hard toward the axis or the point of maximum tension in a phrase, but at that very point you're simply standing there, the most relaxed person in the whole hall. I thought, how wonderful — standing at the crux of this phrase, liberating it.

There are various other insights a pianist can garner from conducting. For instance, a pianist looks at speed with practical considerations — can my fingers work at that speed? Will that be a real problem for that difficult passage? But a conductor frees up such dimensions when she or he looks at the overall picture and thinks about the whole orchestra. Speed is abstracted rather than conceived of in a mechanical or technical way. So, going back to the piano, you wonder: Can I also forget some instrumental restrictions? Free up myself and create new things?

But having said that, there is one big temptation that the conductor faces and which the pianist can learn from: the refusal to let go of a beautiful note. And that's dangerous; music has an inner pulse that should not be distorted too much. Thankfully, that's not a temptation for the pianist: turns out sustaining notes for a long time is not our forte.

LL: How interesting. And I suppose the picture got even more colorful when you also worked with singers at the same time.

CY: Oh, the singers — we spent a lot of time with them. They had such different concerns, you wouldn't be able to imagine. Walking into the hall, you get questions such as "Can you hear every note of my scale?", or "How is my high C today?", or even "What do you think of my vibrato?" They are so concerned with their individual lines, even when singing duets. And all these little things heighten your sensitivity to piano phrasing. When you have different lines or voices in your piano piece, you start wondering if you can give different characters or personalities to each of them. When you play a chord, you start wondering: can I hear the middle note? What about, can I sustain it forever? What is the emotion here?

They are such endearing colleagues, the singers.

LL: I can only try to imagine. It seems to me that such insights refresh the way we think about phrasing chiefly by liberating our preconceived notions of what we can or cannot do with our instrument.

CY: And also expanding your imagination of the sound it can produce; after all, music makes us creative. Richter, for instance, sometimes chooses incredulously slow tempi, especially in Schubert.

Incredulously slow, yes, but also incredibly beautiful.

Chapter 3

Make It New!

3.1 How Does the Pianist Create?

LL: Let's start by picking up from where we last stopped — that music makes us creative. I want to understand this word a little more concisely: Does being creative here mean being imaginative and putting our own personal input into the music? And if so, how do we gauge the amount of creative license we have in making new interpretations of classical music?

CY: These are good questions, but let's frame them in a different way. Instead of asking how much personal input we can put into the music, we can ask: How does the music speak to me? Likewise, instead of asking how much creative license we have in making new interpretations, we might ask: How best can I convey the message of this piece?

These formulations might appear to be two sides of the same coin, a switch from the active to the passive voice, but they are not. The difference in attitude is fundamental.

LL: Do you mean to say that creativity only enters the picture after a thorough understanding of the music?

CY: It might not be wise, or practical, to separate things in this fashion. The role of the classical pianist is quite complex; let me try to explain this in the simplest terms.

Any score that you hold in your hands is written by a specific person, at a specific moment in time, with a specific purpose, in a specific form, for a specific instrument, in a specific musical style, set within a specific historical context — a work is linked to a composer who cannot be divorced from his or her surroundings. So, one of the first steps toward performing a piece of music is to understand the contexts of its creation, and from there, to gradually grasp the composer's world — his or her style, instrumental choices, thoughts, behavior.

In this respect, the performer can be seen as a messenger for the composer; the performance is a medium to convey what the performer perceives as the composer's message to the audience. It is through this conveying — a precise and well formulated recreation of the music, as it were — that the performer's input becomes very important. The performance is no longer just a vehicle to realize the notes on the score; it becomes an interpretation of a piece of music, of a composer's world.

LL: And what precisely is this input on the performer's part? Does it concern exposing certain details or ambiguities in the music in newer, yet ultimately informed ways, or is it about the performer's personality entering the music and shaping it in a more profound way?

CY: Let me share with you an anecdote that might go some way in addressing your question. Back when I was studying at the Royal College — this was in the 50s — I chanced upon Arthur Rubinstein's recordings of the Chopin mazurkas. I put it on, and for its entire duration, I moved not an inch — I was completely entranced. Nothing like it. I sat in silence for a while after it ended, moved yet dumbstruck by the profoundly new meanings that the word "mazurka" now had for me. It was a completely new world.

A good interpreter not only transforms a single piece of music, but also impacts the ways in which we have been conditioned to understand certain forms or rhythms, or even a composer's temperament and his world. But what exactly did Rubinstein do in this recording? Was it his personality or his deep understanding of the mazurkas that made the difference? I don't think we can clearly divide the two. Suffice it to say that a Rubinstein recording will always bear the marks of his personal style, yet it never usurps the musical message of whatever he is playing — he enhances it, communicates it, becomes part of it.

Rubinstein changed the ways we hear Chopin, just as Chopin changed the ways we hear Rubinstein.

3.2 The Case of the Mazurkas

LL: That you can remember this so well after close to 60 years reveals how striking it must have been for you. Can you say a bit more about what Rubinstein's recording did to your understanding of the mazurka?

CY: Rubinstein's strength lies in his ability to unravel the nuances of the mazurka bit by bit. You might think you've garnered the flavor of this dance form by the third or fourth mazurka, but he brings in new surprises each time, a little click of the feet here, a different treatment of the triplet there, so many different colors, rhythms, energies. The listening experience is comparable to reading a really good book, or personally, reading an excellent *wuxia* (Chinese martial heroes) novel — being absorbed into a completely different world propelled by an intricately woven cast of characters. What is he going to do next? What's coming up next? You just cannot stop.

To give you a clearer understanding of Rubinstein's interpretive ability and the craft of playing mazurkas in general, perhaps we can be more specific about the word "mazurka." How do you understand this word?

LL: Well, the mazurka is . . . a flat Polish cake with a shortcrust base — Nela Rubinstein has a nice recipe for it in her cookbook! But as for the kind of mazurka that her husband played: in my impression it's a dance in triple meter with emphases on the second or third beats, unlike the waltz which typically stresses the first. It seems to me that Chopin's mazurkas have a strong folk-inspired element to them in the use of rhythmic patterns, modal sounds, and repetitions. And I find them very difficult to play indeed.

CY: Why are they difficult?

LL: It's hard to know where the stress of the beat falls. My playing always sounds a little lopsided, as if my dancer was always about to fall, never really managing to execute those turns and twirls gracefully. In addition, some of the phrases are really long with repeating motifs, so I struggle to make them sound interesting and convincing. In short, sometimes I just don't know what to do with the notes even though I can play them.

CY: It's interesting you talk about not knowing what to "do with the notes." The performer, Horowitz once said, must find out the music behind the notes, and *do something to it*. "The worst thing is not to do anything. It may even be something you don't like, but do it!"[1]

Each Chopin mazurka comprises a *series* of dances, sometimes so tightly yet gracefully interwoven that your dancer might suddenly find him or herself in a completely different mood, tapping to a very different rhythmic pattern with a turn of the bar. So, the next time you listen to Rubinstein, move from the

---

[1] Elyse Mach, *Great Contemporary Pianists Speak for Themselves* (Chelmsford, MA: Courier Corporation, 1991), p. 116.

general impressions to focus on how he convincingly weaves these contrasting dances together in a single mazurka. The interstices between phrases, the transitions between tunes, the exact timing of the silences between sections, what the listener doesn't actively pay attention to — these are very artful elements that contribute to a good interpretation.

From there, you can start to pay attention to the varying nuances of the different dance melodies in a single mazurka. Now, any pianist who wants to play the mazurkas would have found out that Chopin drew inspiration from the folk music of Mazovia, with considerable emphasis on three contrasting couple dances: the *mazur*, *kujawiak*, and *oberek*. These dances have different characteristics that inspire a whole range of emotions: the irregular accents of the more temperamental *mazur*, the lyricism of the slower *kujawiak*, the exuberance of the repetitive *oberek* (and this is probably the dance whose turns and twirls your dancer struggles with). And underlying all these contrasts is a simultaneous sense of onward momentum and a general tendency to end or lift off the phrase on the second beat, giving a sense of nonfinality.

In fact, when I first learnt how to dance mazurkas during my student days (I was living with a Polish couple), I was struck by how the impetus of the dance was generated by the bar rather than the individual beats, leaving a lot of room for the improvisation of steps. This, in part, contributed to what I felt was a very attractive sense of abandon in the mazurka. In fact, it seems Chopin played his mazurkas with such rhythmic flexibility that the pianist Charles Hallé once remarked to Chopin that he seemed to play the mazurkas in 4/4 rather than 3/4 time. To this, Berlioz would flatly add, "Chopin could not play strictly in time."[2]

---

[2] Frederick Niecks, *Frederick Chopin as a Man and Musician*, Vol. 2 (Frankfurt am Main: Creative Media Partners, reprinted 2018, first published 1888), p. 96.

Regardless of how he really played them, it is undeniable that Chopin pushed the miniature mazurka form into something very ambitious: he incorporated some fugal textures, fragmented lines, and extensive codas showcasing dissonances and startling new melodic material. The mazurka became, for Chopin, a very rich and imaginative form to integrate folk culture from his country and classical music structures; this ties in strongly with how the mazurka was itself a dance form that stretched from its bohemian roots to aristocratic circles.

Now, what should a pianist do with all this information? In fact, there's *too much* to do, so you'd have to choose what you want to do and how to piece all these together like a convincing narrative. After all, the listener wants a journey through these worlds, not a scholarly exposition to them.

LL: Can you show me precisely how such a journeying can be conveyed using a specific example?

CY: Sure, why don't you suggest a mazurka that we can look at?

LL: I really like the mazurka in C-sharp Minor, op. 50 no. 3.

CY: This is an exquisite mazurka, embracing many of the salient characteristics of the dance. Let's just look at the opening bars and see what we can do with them (Figure 1).

First, observe the use of the F double-sharp in the opening theme (circled, first note of bar 2). This sharpened fourth already alerts us to the influence of the Lydian mode,[3] which is

---

[3] The Lydian mode is the common name for the fifth of the eight Gregorian modes, also known as the authentic mode on F, often approximated today as a major scale with the fourth degree raised (for instance, if you play all the white keys from an F to the higher F, you will have an F Major scale with a B-natural rather than a B-flat).

Figure 1: Bars 1–16 of Chopin's Mazurka in C-sharp Minor, op. 50 no. 3. The two important notes discussed, F double-sharp and B-sharp, are circled.

very common in the mazurkas and other Polish folksongs. Here, it serves a very expressive function, lifting the phrase into a rather poignant turn before it resolves temporarily in the third bar. The entry of the second phrase by the left hand is much more confident and assertive: not only does it enter markedly with an accent — somewhat detracting from the opening phrase — it is clipped at 3 bars. Note that the right-hand phrase is, in fact, 5 bars long; the entry of the left hand had delayed its eventual resolution. From these opening bars, we can already observe the dynamic interaction of phrases, further enhanced by very small colorful details in tonality and rhythm.

The second line of the music (bars 9–16) colors this impression with a bright wash of personality, momentum, and expanse. Take a look at the right hand: it's one long phrase with undulating climbs and falls, a touch of rhythmic vibrance with the triplets, a sense of space, and resonance in the closing bars. But note a small detail that concerns the entrance of the right hand: clearly, it starts from the first note of bar 9, the B-sharp (second circle), but this is also clearly marked as the last note of the previous phrase. This very subtle overlap dovetails the

Figure 2:   Bars 17–24 of Chopin's mazurka in C# minor, Op. 50 No. 3, which showcases the impassioned *mazur* theme. The rests and triplets discussed are circled.

dance fragment with the preceding polyphonic material, giving us both a sense of continuity and permutation. Further, the left hand, which primarily provides the dominant pedal in this passage, punctuates the long phrase of the right hand with the lifting of the sustaining pedal — as if giving the long dance sequence small whiffs of air.

LL: And how do we lead this on to the following *mazur* section?

CY: Play on the dramatic contrasts of the two sections. The *mazur* explodes into the scene unapologetically, very much a gush of rapture, nothing like the opening passage we've just seen (Figure 2).

The tightness of the dotted rhythm and the profusion of the accents play a significant role in creating this atmosphere and strong momentum. Note that accents in mazurkas tend to have a larger range of implications than pure emphases. In mimicking the dancer's tap, or a click or kick of the feet, accents often serve to display or punctuate, and can sometimes take a little more time.

There are three features in this theme that can enrich your interpretation. First, the use of rests in bars 18 and 22: Why did Chopin put the rests there when they cannot be heard with the sustaining pedal? Why not just indicate the first note in each bar as a dotted quaver instead? Perhaps these are rests not to be heard but to be felt: instead of holding the first note down, you lift your hands slightly, punctuating the dance with a light, imperceptible uplift before landing slightly delayed. The second beat acts like a cushion, a small intermediate step, before the dancer kicks off again on the third beat with an accent, crossing the bar into the resounding bass notes.

This brings in the second feature: short phrase markings that traverse two bars, typically from the second or third beat of a bar into the first beat of the next. We've just mentioned how the third accented beat of bar 18 seems to leap into the first beat of bar 19 as reflected by the crossbar phrase marking. In bar 19, the right-hand melody does a little turn — interjected by the strong oomph of the bass on the second beat — and crosses into the first beat of bar 20, almost without strict time. These crossbar phrasings give a certain amount of fluidity between the beats and increase the momentum of the music. Imagine your hands, like the dancing couple, running together into the next bar with that simultaneous sense of release and dynamic coordination — an effect enhanced by the simple and intuitive pedaling markings which greatly exploit piano sonority.

The third feature also enhances this enthralling musical momentum: triplets. We've already encountered them in the right hand of the opening passage (Figure 1, bars 10 and 12), but the way the triplets are played in both cases ought to be differentiated. In the opening passage, the triplets can be slightly stretched out to enhance the overarching, undulating 8-bar phrase shape, but in the *mazur* section, they are likely to be squeezed together to give the rhythmic tightness that the lively dance demands. So, just like how accents can convey a range of meanings within a single mazurka, the same can be said of triplets.

Figure 3:   Bars 41–49 of Chopin's Mazurka in C-sharp Minor, op. 50 no. 3, with the playful *oberek* section entering in bar 45. The chords discussed below are circled.

LL: These are indeed very small details that have completely missed my eye. And what advice would you give to interpreting the *oberek* section, which is perhaps what first drew me to this piece?

CY: Why don't you first tell me what about the *oberek* attracted you so?

LL: I adore its highly playful, almost quirky character. I'm also very much attracted to highly repetitive patterns, which the *oberek* certainly does not lack.

CY: The *oberek* section is indeed very charming, and I think you'd be quite capable of expressing its character once you break it down further. Let's take a quick look at it (Figure 3).

Already from these first few bars of the *oberek*, we can detect a small detail that can go a long way in helping us shape the whirling repeated patterns of the entire section: a very subtle chord change. Look at bars 45 and 47 — the chord in the third beat encompasses a very small change from the preceding and following harmony, but that very subtle change actually swerves the tonic chord into the subdominant, giving that third beat a bit more stress and tension. Giving this detail due notice will also give you more insight into the punctuative function of the sustaining pedal as indicated.

LL: From your detailed analysis, it seems to me that a large part of musical interpretation lies in discovering and making sense of very small details hidden in the score, the way a poetry scholar might break down and reveal all sorts of sound patterns that make up the poem's construction.

CY: Indeed, but bear in mind that the pianist must then weave all these details and connections together into a convincing whole. To do this without obscuring the coherence and immediacy of the notes you're playing at that precise moment is quite a challenge. If you were to give the Rubinstein recording a good listen, you'd realize that his interpretive strength lies in emphasizing and contrasting minute colorful features of each mazurka, resulting in a dazzling impression of the dance form when heard as a collection. But another performer can do something completely different and still come up with an excellent interpretation. For instance, Horowitz in his 1969 recording of this mazurka plays the opening bars with much broader brush strokes — the contrapuntal texture is less strongly emphasized, the chords in the left hand are more pedaled, you can almost drive a steady pulse through the 16 bars, something that is impossible with Rubinstein's. The effect is mesmerizing and nostalgic.

LL: How striking — the amount of precision and planning that goes into every note of the music, yet it all sounds natural and almost intuitive to the listener.

CY: There are so many attractive interpretations at our disposal today, all lying in wait for our discovery. If you listened carefully and widely enough, these myriad interpretations would reveal to you how truly international Chopin's language is — for something rather different from Horowitz's and Rubinstein's, you may give Fou Ts'ong's recordings a listen. His rendition of that C-sharp Minor mazurka is almost a full minute slower than Rubinstein's or Horowitz's, full of subtlety and sensitivity, offering us new inspiration and fresh meaning. Or what about Ignaz Friedman? Listening to his utterly effortless, vivacious mazurka recordings made some 90 years ago might impress on you how Chopin's music transcends so many barriers.

Coming up with your own interpretation of a piece takes time, skill, resourcefulness, and a fair dosage of self-awareness. To develop your own musical personality, Rubinstein once told a young student, you need to listen to both yourself and other pianists with a critical ear, keeping and adopting what you like, and rejecting what you dislike. "The bee flies from flower to flower and tries to find her best mixture in creating her honey, so try to make your musical honey the same way," he said.[4]

3.3 Can the Pianist Create Mistakenly?

LL: It seems to me that despite all these good intentions there remains the possibility that an interpretation has certain characteristics that might make a listener react, "That's good, but it doesn't really sound like Chopin." How does that happen?

CY: If the pianist had indeed done everything we've mentioned above, then he or she will find other listeners who have no problems with the interpretation. Let me share an anecdote with you by way of illustration.

I was examining a student with a colleague. The playing was not fantastic, but neither was it poor — this usually poses more problems for examiners. The point of contention was the student's rendition of a Beethoven sonata; my colleague was rather inclined to fault him for his interpretation. I did not reveal what I thought immediately; instead, I posed a series of questions to figure out what he didn't like.

Were there many wrong notes? No, he said. Was the playing insecure? No, I wouldn't think so. Was it distracting? No, not at all. If

---

[4] Harvey Sachs, *Rubinstein: A Life* (New York, NY: Grove Press, 1995), p. 335.

this piece was not written by Beethoven, is it disagreeable? No . . . not really. Did he have something to say? Yes, I would say so . . .

You can see where this is going. After a while, there's nothing left to be said — the playing is neither disagreeable nor incompetent. Just because the student does not play your kind of Beethoven does not mean he cannot stand his ground; in an examination where personal preference does not play the determining role, the student certainly does not deserve to fail.

Having said that, it doesn't mean that *any* rendition of Beethoven works. You can't play this Beethoven scale the same way you would in a Mozart sonata — different styles, different circumstances. Any good interpretation must incorporate scholarship, industry, self-awareness, and resourcefulness. Only by respecting the tradition can you try to challenge it.

LL: So, the fact that your colleague could disagree strongly with the student's interpretation of Beethoven despite its overall competence — does that boil down to taste? "That student was playing Beethoven competently enough, but it was altogether in bad taste?"

CY: Taste is a vague and personal thing. A listener's taste for certain sounds or personalities — say a rich sound over a bright sound, or a wash of grandeur over a more intimate treatment — may shape his or her preference for a performer over the other. But a good listener would not let taste occlude an appreciation of any performer's interpretation if it is competently executed. An interpretation that is sure-footed in its treatment of the music within scholarship would not be put down by subjective tastes; you need not love it, but you can still admire its craft. To put it in everyday terms, surely you can admire a *pisang goreng*[5] deep fried to the highest degree of perfection, even if you prefer to eat bananas raw?

---

[5] A banana fritter snack commonly found in Southeast-Asia.

LL: Surely. A good *pisang goreng* enhances the flavor of the banana beyond its raw form, but there are so many ways that a *pisang goreng* can go wrong that a raw banana cannot — above all, tasting the oil rather than the banana.

CY: Here we're getting somewhere interesting. A greasy *pisang goreng* is no longer about taste, is it? When a performance presents certain elements that detracts from the musical material   certain habits that pervade the way of playing, for instance — then we're talking about mannerisms rather than interpretations. A performance that presents pervasive mannerisms is, first and foremost, an inadequate performance before it can be discussed as an interpretation of anything.

LL: What are some examples of these mannerisms and how can we guard against them?

CY: Mannerisms creep in all the time in everything we do. Take everyday speech. You may have a friend who likes to start every sentence with "you know" or peppers every other phrase with "like." Are these ways of speaking irritating *per se*? Not really — they can be charming, unique, even endearing, but when these habits are excessive and become pervasive mannerisms, there are larger consequences. The listener starts to become distracted by the manner of speech rather than the message of the speech, the content is occluded, even existing positive aspects of the delivery might be obliterated.

The examples at the piano are just as numerous. When you first came to me, you used to prolong rests rather frequently, especially if they contributed to the closure of the phrase — this is a kind of mannerism that distorts the momentum of the music. Or a typical example: a student, much enthused by Chopin, might start pedaling through the repertoire or using rubato indiscriminately. Why is that to be discouraged? Because some pieces need stability rather than flexibility; when you have a rest in Bach, you want to hear it rather than feel it the way you would in Debussy — like a kind of transparency. Yet another student took to starting phrases with an accent and tapering them off. I asked him: Have you been playing some jazz lately?

How do we guard against mannerisms? Well, you sought my help. Every student can benefit from a teacher, and a teacher might have a helpful colleague. But above all, listen to others, and yourself, and be self-critical. "I call my records the only real teachers I ever had," Rubinstein once revealed in a letter.[6]

3.4 Does the Pianist Create Something New?

LL: I want to pause at this moment and assemble everything we've said. Suppose I hold a new score in my hands. First, I study it, do a close analysis, and formulate, in my own terms, what it is saying. I bolster my initial interpretation with knowledge about the composer's contexts. After I can play it according to my own interpretation, I look to other existing recordings for inspiration, critically adopting or rejecting certain elements in my own playing. My overarching aim is to convey, in a coherent and interesting fashion, what I think are the most important elements of the composer's message. Further, I should guard against mannerisms in my playing that might detract from conveying this message.

It seems to me, at this point, that the pianist as an interpreter doesn't actually create anything new. Rather, he or she is trying to be an accurate, contemporary extension of the composer.

CY: What you've said is understandable, if somewhat pessimistic. Richter went further: in his eyes, the interpreter did not truly

---

[6] Sachs, p. 334.

exist — he or she was just a mirror that reflected the score as accurately as possible.[7] Yet we can recognize Richter's sound from miles away.

Is this a conundrum? I don't think so. Let's unravel this by way of an example — why don't you tell me something you're playing now?

LL: This might sound slightly surprising, but I'm looking at Schumann's Fantasy in C again, specifically the third movement.

CY: How do you find it this time? It must have been more than six years since you last played it.

LL: It's bizarre. Six years ago, I really struggled to find a connection with the third movement, which had seemed to me so disconnected with the first two movements; it was highly inaccessible and seemed to go on forever with no real purpose. I could still put everything together with a semblance of musical sense, but emotionally I did not feel anything. Now I find that every note in there has a place, the key modulations are nothing less than magical, and the musical message is truly pressing and poignant. This situation seems bizarre to me because I finally feel there's something I can say with this piece, and I definitely didn't get here by way of practice or extensive research.

CY: There's an insight that we can gain from your experience: the starting point into a work, that initial encounter between an interpreter and a score, can greatly shape the interpretation. Typically, a performer plays the same work throughout his or her life with many versions; the work may be the same, but the performer's initiation into the work can take place under different circumstances of understanding and experience.

---

[7] Bruno Monsaingeon, *Sviatoslav Richter: Notebooks and Conversations* (Princeton, NJ: Princeton University Press, 2001), p. xv.

This produces remarkably different interpretations, and it's a good example of how an interpreter's input does create, time and again, something new out of the same score — the music behind the notes gain a different narrative each time, a new light if you like.

But there's so much more than an interpreter can create and does create. Take humor. Can there be humor in music? When pianists strive to recreate the musical message behind the notes, some will find ways to convey humor and others not. And what kind of humor? There are so many strains and degrees of humor that can be discovered and conveyed: it could be the contrast of registers and articulation in the fashion of slapstick humor, or something more deep-seated like Prokofiev's irony. And this, again, is an active role of interpretation that creates new and unexpected dimensions to understanding and enjoying music.

And this ties in to what can be seen as the gift of a truly remarkable interpreter: the ability to bring together all these disparate fragments and convey the music like a story to the audience. Mind you, the interpreter would have rehashed this story to him or herself countless times through practice but will still be able to convey it to the audience during the performance or the recording as if it is a story the first time told. He or she will be able to bring us through the surprise of a counter-melody, the remarkable arc of the motif the first time heard, the strange familiarity of a transposed theme, the dizzying liberation of the mazurka's *oberek*.

And that could very well be the greatest challenge and invention of the interpreter.

Part 2
Behind the Grace Note

Chapter 4

Please Don't Shoot the Student

4.1 Teaching, Discovering

CY: I received a postcard from a former student yesterday. It's probably been decades since I last heard from him. I remember him well — a splendid performer, and now a very good teacher in the States. Time flies; it's nice to hear from your students now and again.

LL: It must be rewarding to know that your teaching has benefitted many pianists who have themselves become good teachers to a future generation of pianists.

CY: Indeed, I think every professional will have the desire, at some point in his or her life, to pass down knowledge and experience to the next generation. But developing a good pianist is quite different from developing a good teacher; teaching is not a natural extension of performing. I see teaching as almost a different profession. Your starting point is different, your approach must be flexible, your aims are manifold.

LL: In your opinion, what is one of the most fundamental aspects of teaching music?

CY: Finding the optimal combination of exercises, challenges, and repertoire — the right diet — for each student is fundamental, and sometimes quite challenging. There are four main aspects to this.

The first is to make sure that you give the student a balanced diet. There should be no extremes and fanatic aims involved; having exposure to just one or two composers will limit the student's musical development. Only with a broad exposure can the student pick up different techniques that the music demands, and in the process absorb a wide range of sounds, tonalities, and rhythms.

From this exposure, the teacher will be able to grasp what the student is good at, enjoys doing, or has problems playing. This is where the second step comes in: exploiting the strengths and tackling the weaknesses. For instance, if the student has a fantastic sense of rhythm, give pieces that will allow him or her to show these abilities; the boost in confidence and enjoyment at the piano is important in the learning process. At the same time, however, you must pair this with material to sharpen what he or she is weak in — do not skirt around the problem!

Third, the teacher needs to constantly expand the student's horizon by putting challenges in place. How to design these challenges takes skill, patience, and experience: you want to make the challenge just a notch beyond what the student is comfortable, so that she or he gets there almost without knowing it. This is especially important when you have talented students who tend to overexert and risk sustaining injuries when they face difficult challenges. For this reason, setting systematically tiered challenges acts as a protective measure. This third step is quite important because you want to encourage the student to have his or her input in the learning process — actively achieving a goal and attaining a sense of achievement increases his or her involvement in the process.

And lastly, the teacher needs to create occasions for the student to show off his or her ability. Do not underestimate the importance of this sense of occasion to the learner, even if she or he happens to be extremely shy; if a student concert is too grand a stage, you could simply consider having him or her first demonstrate to another student.

LL: This certainly sounds like a great deal of attention and time devoted to every single student! Is this why some pianists might consider teaching as somewhat detrimental to a performing career?

CY: Teaching does not take away from performance *per se*; there is no conflict between the two. But as you've seen, it does take away time and energy, and when something must give, it's usually teaching that is sacrificed.

Perhaps it's more interesting to examine the difference between the two. Consider that you're both performing and teaching the Debussy *Préludes*. As a teacher, it might be tempting to simply show the student how you would play it. But learning at an advanced stage is scarcely about imitation; the teacher must not aim to simply reproduce copies of him or herself! Instead, the teacher has to discover the student — every student.

What does that mean? At its most basic level, you must start from the student's point of view and understand the composition of his or her musical diet. If he or she has never played Debussy, then starting with the *Préludes* might be too big a challenge, leading to a dip in morale or even overexertion. This might seem an obvious oversight, but sometimes teachers make mistakes too, and starting from your own repertoire for the student is a common one. Or take a different scenario: if the student has small hands, then using your fingering for a difficult passage might make things even harder. The teacher must investigate different alternatives, including some which she or he might never fathom using personally.

So, broadly speaking, a teacher must try to understand why a student faces particular difficulties even when, and *especially* when, those are not problems that the teacher faces. In guiding the student to find his or her own unique solutions, the teacher helps the student develop skills that will extend beyond the learning of that single piece.

LL: This approach of "guiding the student to find his or her own solutions" I wholeheartedly agree with, but I find it especially challenging to translate to practical terms. Can you explain it a little further?

CY: I'd give you an example, albeit one that is a little extreme. There were three of us young pianists who had been selected to perform the Chopin B Minor sonata for a series of six masterclasses in Siena with Agosti. The sonata was not in my repertoire, so it was a bit of a rush to learn it. We each played the sonata in turn. Agosti shook his head, no no no, not so good, he said. All we received were negative comments: too fast, too slow; too loud, too soft; unclear punctuation, misplaced climaxes; stiff phrasing, mundane pedaling; insensitive balance, unimaginative voicing . . . the list went on. After 18 hours of masterclass I still had no idea how exactly I ought to play this sonata.

Understandably, I was rather upset; I was hoping to get some input to eventually perform the piece. But why did he do that? Then it struck me. His message may be implicit, and its delivery downright frustrating, but it was full of imagination and conviction. His point was: here are 2000 ways how *not* to play this sonata; you must find your own unique way. In other words, he took care to only show us elements that weakened or detracted from our playing, leaving each of us to find out, in our own time, how we wanted to make sense of the acceptable bits that remained.

Chances are you're not going to do this to your student — anyone other than Agosti delivering that masterclass might be labeled a bad teacher. But use the underlying principle and help your students to find their own interpretations with their own resources. For instance, you can link the student's piano playing to another aspect of his or her life, and further, to other strengths that she or he may have. Helping the student see music in a different light might offer new insights and solutions. Take a student who finds a certain piano phrase rather difficult to shape. If you link it to his or her interest in conducting, then the solutions might suddenly seem numerous. This is because a phrase wears a rather different cloak under the conductor's baton; a pianist might be preoccupied with the physical aspect of delivering the phrase, but a conductor will have different concerns such as "what timbre do I have here?" or "where do I place the balance of the music at this precise point?". These connections broaden the student's perspective of a phrase in both piano playing and conducting. Or suppose you have a student who is a good dancer — some imaginative cross-referencing to his or her strengths can inspire those difficult leaps, turns, and rhythms to become expressive and even liberating on the piano.

LL: And would you say that such imaginative and implicit guidance to help the student find his or her own solution might not work as well for certain student groups? For instance, it seems to me that young children already have an excess of imagination at the piano, and it is the teacher who must find a way to shape or direct this imagination without curbing it.

CY: Indeed, given that young children approach piano playing in a completely different way from mature students, teachers should also adapt their teaching to draw on and, in turn, build on these different strengths. This entails a rather fundamental change of perspective on the teacher's part.

When a young child puts his or her hands down on the piano, it is most often the case that something extremely funny comes out: a splattering of sounds, a fistful of notes, and — very often — a smack of black keys. This, in fact, is not all that surprising: Chopin realized that the black keys not only provided much better geography on the keyboard than the white keys, they also encouraged the hand to stay in a more natural, relaxed position. This led him to introduce the B Major scale as the first right hand scale and the D-flat Major as the first left hand scale for the young pianist, leaving the hardest — C Major — to the last, very much contrary to contemporary pedagogy![1]

The innocent, natural attitude that children have toward the piano reveals the lack of prior knowledge, configurations, norms — things that often completely catch the teacher off guard. Instead of putting down these intuitive actions immediately, start precisely from the positive attributes of their lack. If you have a large chord, can you not imagine the vast space that separates the notes? How about the monstrosity that *overwhelms* those dissonant chords? A young child might not know the composers and their contexts, but she or he will still be able to produce different sounds from a single chord or a vast array of sounds associated with certain types of pieces. The focus here is fun and enjoyment; without knowing it, the student develops certain abilities and ways of listening before she or he is ready to incorporate knowledge about contexts and traditions.

LL: It seems to me that your approach to teaching places a strong emphasis on discovering the individual strengths, personalities, and backgrounds of each student rather than imparting knowledge. How did you come to formulate such an approach?

---

[1] Eigeldinger, pp. 34–37.

CY: I'd start by saying that this is the approach I adopt, but it's not the only one that works, and it certainly wasn't the predominant approach back in my time. It used to be the case that a student's interpretation, style, or tone could quite easily give away who his or her teacher was; a student's performance was quite directly a product of the teacher. I believe, however, in helping students develop their personalities through their own responses to the music; the performance can only partly be said to be my product in terms of meeting a certain professional standard or quality.

In this respect, the Confucian value "因材施教" (yin cai shi jiao) is what inspires and underpins my approach: to teach according to an individual's aptitude. To carry this out, however entails a huge amount of time, energy, and thought spent on every single student that you decide to take on.

LL: Can you give me an example in which this approach seemed to be especially important or helpful to a student?

CY: I had a student who was almost completely blind. This did not create major difficulties in interpreting and performing pieces, for he had excellent physical sense and musical aptitude, but it did make learning pieces quite tedious. So, I concentrated on helping him learn pieces — a step in the learning process which all advanced students are expected to fulfill independently before they show up for classes. This meant investigating the most intuitive hand positionings, fingerings, patterns, and arm movements for him to learn the pieces quickly and securely, in addition to increasing his geographical grasp of the keyboard by physically guiding his hands across the keys.

4.2 Learning, Questioning

LL: You mention that your teaching approach stems from a strong belief in "因材施教," but might it also have been influenced by your own experience as a piano student? I understand that you've been coached by many outstanding pianists and teachers in your life, among them, Julius Katchen, Kendall Taylor, Magda Tagliaferro. Did they also share this approach, and if not, how did you cope with their different schools of teaching?

CY: Every teacher brings a vast range of elements to your plate, including some which you might intuitively disagree with. Pursue this discord not by conflict but by inquiry: instead of saying that you think otherwise, find out why your teacher thinks that way. The answer might give you a great deal of insight — it might even reveal that it was an obscured perspective that led to your initial reaction.

In this sense, I've never in any lesson voiced my disagreement, but I've always very critically questioned everything I was taught: Can I do it better? How can I play it differently? This was how I benefitted under contrasting teaching approaches — from elements that were both inspiring and seemingly disagreeable. And elements that were practically disagreeable I found my ways around: there was no way I would practice just technique for six months when I had to give concerts. I did not say; my teacher ostensibly did not find out.

Take another example. One teacher might think that a young pianist should stay away from big works, such as the last Beethoven sonatas, until she or he matures or gains some life experiences to understand the complexities of the work. Another might say that a pianist should grow with such a work, benefitting precisely from the various entry points influenced by age and experience. This difference in approach is not uncommon: when I played Beethoven's op. 111 at my Wigmore Hall debut, my former teacher almost died from shock.

There's always much to gain from various teachers. Their differences do not create a discord with which to cope, but rather a productive contrast from which you benefit through questioning and amalgamating; this makes learning music a very exciting journey. But having said that, there are circumstances under which questioning might not be that beneficial to learning.

LL: What are these circumstances?

CY: First, time. When time is a limiting factor, questioning might not be the most productive way forward. I'd give you an example. I once observed two students performing at a masterclass. The master took very well to one of them but thought rather critically of the other, brusquely putting down many aspects of her playing. The latter was rather stumped and approached me after the class: Why did the master have a rather binary approach to pedaling? Why would she place such a strong emphasis on note articulation rather than phrase shaping? Valid as these questions may be, I asked her in turn: But could you execute what she wanted you to do on the spot? Could you immediately adapt your playing, and your mindset, to her criticism? If you couldn't, then you need to work on yourself first.

Because time is a limiting factor in a masterclass, a student should take the opportunity to adapt as quickly as possible to the master's criticism rather than question it. Such is the perfect setting to train your ability to quickly harness your resources — technique, perspective, spontaneity — under time pressure; this flexibility and quick-thinking will help you in your performing career.

This brings me to a second point on questioning: always know what you can offer from the position you question. If there's something you question because you disagree with it, inform your grounds of disagreement by grasping, as much as you can, both the opposing view and your own alternatives. This is why pianists who are just starting off, gaining exposure to different approaches and finding their own sound might consider holding off their questions.

LL: Given that the pianists who once coached you had varying approaches to both teaching and playing the piano — for instance, Agosti, a disciple of Busoni, clearly contrasted Tagliaferro, whose French school lineage stretched to Chopin through Cortot — how were your takeaways from their classes different?

CY: Agosti, for all his teaching of how not to play the Chopin sonata, was a master at carving a single phrase. It was quite extraordinary, but the onus was on the student to find out how to integrate these exquisite phrasing details into the overall interpretation of a single piece. If every phrase was accorded such luxurious treatment, the piece will sound like a meal of chocolate — too much, too rich.

Kendall Taylor was a very different teacher. For my first lesson, he advocated a series of exercises and movements; to him, a musician must be systematic in building his or her foundation to enable freer expression at a later stage. One principle he insisted on was rhythmic cohesion: too much rhythmic freedom and the piece risks breaking apart.

As for Tagliaferro, she had a remarkable way of teaching. For every lesson she'd be armed with a whole set of different colored pencils, each color symbolizing a different concern: green, for instance, might refer to tempo refinements, blue to phrasing indications, and so on, and red resolutely meant that a mistake had been made. At her hands, scores sometimes turned into drawings of sorts! She always had a very positive, no-nonsense attitude: every technique had to be analyzed leaving no vague corners. Above all, she had a strong conviction in what she delivered — this was something I took away from her.

These pianists were great personalities. I continued to play for Julius Katchen in the 60s, and he only had positive things to say. When Rudolf Serkin arrived to perform in Singapore and Malaysia in 1960 only to learn that a Singaporean pianist was shortly scheduled to play the "Appassionata" too, he spontaneously replaced it with the "Waldstein" for his performance. That he was very encouraging to us young pianists only made me more impressed. He had, by the way, astounding concentration: I listened to him practice the opening G Major chord of Beethoven's fourth piano concerto for two hours.

When a young pianist starts to develop his own personality and career, his or her relationship with mentors will understandably change too. I remember once playing for Kendall Taylor in the 60s, and all he said was: well, for that single phrase you can play it like this, or like this, or even like this (each time demonstrating at the piano what he meant), but certainly not your way. I responded: I'm surprised you now have three interpretations of that phrase! We had a good laugh. No more questions asked.

4.3 Living, Inspiring

LL: We have talked about how an inquisitive learning approach and a flexible and individually catered teaching approach can yield certain positive results in music. Yet, it seems to me that they both demand a prerequisite in the student, one that frequently presents itself as a hurdle in my teaching: discipline. It might be clear to the teacher that a student needs to acquire a certain set of skills and technique before she or he can think about ways of expressing the music; I see this very clearly as learning how to use a tool before speaking about the rewards it can reap. Yet this logic is not necessarily clear to the student, and even if it is, she or he might get impatient, resulting in a lack of discipline to practice. How can I solve this problem?

CY: The problem here is not, in fact, a lack of discipline; it is first a lack of enthusiasm. Instead of asking "how can I make sure she or he practices," ask "how can I inspire him or her to meet a challenge, and in the course of doing so, *want* to practice?" At this point, it is crucial to know the strengths, weaknesses, and personality of your student to know the right kind of challenge to set. Do you set a series of minutely refined challenges, or do you set a large and formidable one? If you have an ambitious and impatient student, then the former approach might have an adverse effect.

Let me give you an example. Suppose a student shows up for class with a work just slightly under-prepared. The first teacher might say "this is not adequate; the lesson ends here." The second teacher might say "for this difficult section, you might consider using these practice methods to smoothen out your problems." It might seem to us that the latter is obviously more constructive and helpful, but in fact, it might turn out that the former suits the ambitious student better. Not only does it instill in the student an alarmingly clear sense of respect for the profession and the self — "never forget that your most basic goal as a student is to arrive for class with a work prepared" — it spurs him or her on to fully utilize lesson time and, therefore, to find ways to make home practice time more productive. In fact, I'd add that sometimes such students who are ambitious and intermittently impatient or restless can become quite enthusiastic if you encourage them to coach other younger students. In wanting to excel in such a setting, they give themselves the impetus to work on their own self-discipline.

When a student shows up for his or her first class with a certain level of enthusiasm for music, it is the teacher's utmost responsibility to increase, or at least, maintain that enthusiasm for the rest of the time the student is under your charge.

In this sense, I set very high standards for my profession: if a student loses that enthusiasm, the teacher has failed. And when you manage to grow that enthusiasm, it is quite likely that your student comes back with different aspirations and ideas, sometimes rather exciting ones, which will further shape and drive your own teaching, sometimes even your musical understanding. I once observed a student presenting to Tagliaferro a Bach piece, very much well-prepared, and after the lesson she closed the score and said, "this is not my Bach, but it's yours — you've convinced me." This shows openness, and more: it shows that learning and teaching could very well be two sides of the same coin.

So, going back to your question: when you face certain problems in discipline, it might prove more useful to find numerous ways to increase the student's enthusiasm for music in a more general sense, rather than to put in place measures to work on discipline *per se*. A lack of discipline is frequently a manifestation of a broader issue that you must learn to discover and tackle accordingly as you go along in the teaching process.

LL: Other than this clear aim of increasing a student's enthusiasm for learning music, are there other broad goals that we can keep in mind in our teaching, especially for students who might not necessarily aspire to be concert pianists?

CY: Entering music is quite different from becoming a world-class performer. You can be so many things in the music profession: a teacher, an accompanist, even a manager. But whatever the student becomes, she or he needs to cultivate the necessary habits and discipline of the mind to enter the profession. For instance, when faced with a complex score, she or he must be able to break it down into simpler elements of analysis before resynthesizing them again. Few elements around us work in isolation, yet we must learn to dissect and categorize things in the hope that we see the whole more clearly; that's the discipline I hope to help students develop not just in the music profession but in life at large.

But more broadly, teaching music far exceeds helping a student refine his or her interpretation of a piece or perfecting certain technical feats; to shape and guide an appreciation of music in its entirety helps an individual develop an awareness or mastery of numerous intellectual and emotional aspects. Plato in the *Republic* looked to music for the education of the soul and gymnastics for the education of the body; by drawing from how an infant relaxes from the rhythm of rocking and the melody of singing, he saw in music a means of emotional comfort and pleasure, directly striking the senses and giving them its shape. This, he believed, indirectly prepares the intellect for learning.

Hence, a music teacher may teach primarily to help a student play an instrument better, but the impact of this teaching — good teaching — can shape the individual's ways of thinking, learning, and feeling at large. Music may begin as a mere speck of interest (and in young students, very often a healthy desire to show off!) but it oftentimes becomes a significant source of recourse and inspiration that follows you for the rest of your life, regardless of whether you enter the profession.

Chapter 5

The Pianist's Dirty Laundry

5.1 Know Your Tool

LL: In our previous conversation, we touched briefly on how technique forms an essential component of a student's musical diet. But teaching technique effectively is not easy — it is repetitive, boring, and only yields results after much sustained practice. This challenge is further enhanced when you have a talented, young student; drilling the fundamental technical exercises seems especially essential to create a solid foundation, but also somewhat detrimental as it curbs the enthusiasm of the child. What is your take on this?

CY: Let's start by understanding the relationship between technique and music. How do you see this relationship?

LL: I see technique as the backbone of musical expression. Without technique, the pianist is not at liberty to fully tap on the characteristics of the instrument to express his or her version of the music.

CY: Indeed, technique serves music, but it is important to also bear in mind that music drives technique. It is the musician's desire to be able to play the full range of music available that propels pedagogues to create systems of technical exercises; whenever this range gets expanded with new sounds or instrumental changes, technique must also quickly adapt itself to accommodate such musical demands.

Drawing upon this relationship, we can formulate two different approaches to technique in your case of the young, talented student. The more traditional school would say that the student should develop technique before approaching repertoire — technique anticipates music; the student who has the self discipline to first master technique will find it much easier when she or he attempts to play pieces. But another school of thought would say that the student can likewise develop a good technical foundation by being exposed to a specially curated range of works; playing such works will present enough technical problems for the student to solve. In this sense, it is music that stimulates technique; the student who diligently strives to solve problems encountered in learning the pieces will, as a result, develop technique.

Both schools of thought have much to offer. But notice that both also demand discipline on the student's part, just at different stages of the learning process. The onus is, thus, on the teacher to find out the stages at which the student is more receptive to being discouraged or being disciplined. Chances are, you'd have to subtly combine both schools in the course of teaching the young student, whose personality, strengths, and weaknesses are also ever evolving.

LL: In this respect, would you say that your approach to technique is very much in line with your teaching philosophy of "因材施教" (to teach according to an individual's aptitude)?

CY: Yes, in the sense that there are many ways to help a student develop technique, of which some are more suited to certain students than others. But also, no, because there are some fundamental aspects of technique that every pianist must develop regardless of their personality, aptitude, or goals of learning music: strong fingers, strong fingertips, and the ability to stretch.

LL: So, are these aspects that must be learned by rote, analogous to how grammar rules and verb conjugations are first memorized when we learn a language?

CY: Learning a language is akin to learning music, but the relationship between grammar and technique is a strenuous one. I do not advocate "learning by rote"; learning should embrace fun and purpose. Technique is primarily physical, and hence, must be taught in alignment with the unique physical attributes of the pianist. In this respect, there are more similarities to be found between the training of a pianist and an athlete.

Let's take football. Now, just about everyone can kick a football — it's a simple and natural action. But can everyone kick the ball equally well with both legs, or score the ball just within the top corners of the goal? A professional footballer makes kicking a football become a physical feat, an act of contortion — likewise a pianist. And the training that leads up to that act draws from the naturalness of kicking a ball or hitting a piano key, but eventually radically departs from that to enhance speed, control, precision, consistency, and endurance under conditions of stress and tension.

And this radical departure sometimes comprises aspects that we won't readily associate with the sport or the craft. For instance, I once observed table tennis players balancing themselves on gymnastic balls as part of their training. Apparently, this improves their sense of balance so that they do not fall in the most awkward situations, or, if they almost do, can quickly adapt and regain their balance. Now, the same can be said of a pianist's training. While pianists don't actually fall off the stool, they are less daring when they feel unbalanced. This especially shows up when executing jumps — you need a sense of stability to make that leap. Hence, establishing a sense of balance is, in fact, of utmost importance from the start of the training; the pianist should learn how to manipulate just three points to feel balanced, with much attention paid to the left foot.

LL: I want to zoom in a little on your point about naturalness — that musical training draws upon the naturalness of certain mechanical movements or physical attributes. Could you elaborate a little more on this with precise examples?

CY: Let's take a few simple and natural movements that we use in everyday life: turning the doorknob, tapping someone on the shoulder, waving goodbye — these are all everyday movements that are natural and highly economical. When developed as piano techniques, they can miraculously reduce tension and cut down injury across repetitive and strenuous passages.

A little flippant perhaps, but it's no exaggeration to say that for a left-handed person, piano playing starts with "turning a doorknob" — pronation, which brings all the fingers in contact with the keys. This subtle rotation takes place constantly in playing the piano and it enables us to play two notes without much effort and tension. "Tapping someone on the shoulder": this gentle movement from the wrist is a tremendous kick-start in preparing us to play staccatos. And "waving goodbye": the lateral hand movement opens doors for us to gulp up distance that we normally cannot reach by stretching, and the lateral forearm movement combined with a swift shift makes us feel that there is no region on the keyboard that we cannot arrive in comfort and style.

Another mechanical movement that the pianist can make use of is the natural drop. Since it utilizes gravity as its force, it naturally releases tension and potentially reinforces tone quality. Curiously, this is an action that we try to eliminate in the playing of young children — since it comes almost too naturally to them — and subsequently try to regain in the advanced stages. At this point, pianists must learn to control the drop by manipulating a few factors: the speed of the drop, the use of the wrist as a shock absorber, the braced fingers as you land. The natural drop gives you color without effort, but it comes with the risk of dropping at the wrong place — a risk that does not exist if you play from the note instead. Hence, make sure that you develop a good geography of the piano — practicing with eyes closed or in the dark can be useful here.

As with most things, use these movements in moderation and never in isolation: there is no need to rotate a scale or execute a dramatic drop for every bass note marked *forte*; likewise, treat with a critical attitude any system that too strongly advocates a single movement above others — it's bound to be too limited. Treat your fingers as a tool that must be cultivated in a systematic, holistic, and grounded fashion so that its full potential can be reached. In this respect, strong and flexible fingers should still very much form the basis of a pianist's technique.

5.2 Pitting Your Tool

LL: At this point, I want to backtrack a little and ask you a few questions about the history of piano technique. I understand that there were distinct schools of piano pedagogy starting from the late seventeenth century and stretching all the way till at least the mid-twentieth century: the major French, German, and Russian schools, and perhaps less distinctly the Italian, American, Polish, and English. Are these schools of pedagogy still relevant today when we think about learning and developing piano technique? For instance, the French school might place more emphasis on developing a *jeu perlé* touch[1] than other traditions.

---

[1] *Jeu perlé* is a kinesthetic style of piano playing that emphasizes rapid and rhythmically regular finger work close to the keys with sparing use of the pedal. The

CY: This is an interesting question, but it requires quite a bit of unpacking. The idea of national piano schools is complex and multifaceted. It revolves around numerous factors such as the emergence of music conservatories, key figures, or pedagogues firmly associated with the lineage of the national school, instrumental manufacture and choices, traditions in choosing performance repertoire, and very broad archetypes associated with the playing style, which are further influenced by factors such as cultural and historical conditioning. Hence, while it is possible to trace how and why these national schools place different emphases on developing and refining certain piano techniques, whether such an investigation will benefit the modern pianist in a practical sense is questionable.

The first thing you must realize is that overarching presumptions about the characteristic techniques and sound of each school can sometimes gloss over finer constituent factors. Let's start our brief exposition from Paris to understand how the technique of *le jeu perlé* came about. One of the key factors that led to the emergence of the French school is the establishment of the Paris Conservatory in 1795; within the next half-century numerous conservatories in Europe and Russia would follow suit, such as the Royal Academy of Music in London in 1822, the Leipzig Conservatory in 1843 (founded by Mendelssohn), and the Moscow Conservatory and Saint Petersburg Conservatory in 1866 and 1862, respectively (led by the Rubinstein brothers).

An important factor to note is that the state-run Paris Conservatory restricted external influences by making French citizenship a prerequisite to study and teach in the piano department — even the 12-year old Liszt (who, after receiving

---

effect is a light and clear sound, wherein notes of a scale sound like individual pearls. It has frequently been discussed with the technique of Saint-Saëns and Marguerite Long among many other French pianists and pedagogues.

instruction from Czerny for a year, had already managed to leave a positive impression on the gloomy Beethoven[2]) was turned down when he applied to be a student in 1823.

Many major French composers of the nineteenth century, in turn, passed through the conservatory — Berlioz was admitted in 1826, Bizet and Saint-Saëns in 1848, Debussy in 1872, Ravel in 1889. When Fauré — student of Saint-Saëns and teacher of Ravel — was appointed director of the conservatory in 1905, he expanded students' repertoire to include contemporary works of the aforementioned composers, sometimes even commissioning new works from them for end-of-year instrumental examinations.

These structural changes went in hand with faculty reformations. Fauré appointed Alfred Cortot and Marguerite Long to be part of the piano department — notably, the former's lineage stretched to Chopin and the latter's directly to Marmontel. Both Cortot and Long were active performers and advocates of the compositions of many contemporary French composers, many of whom were their close friends. Long, for instance, premiered Ravel's Concerto in G in 1932, with the composer precariously conducting. In fact, Ravel had wanted to be the soloist himself, but decided to approach Long two months before the premiere because he realized he couldn't execute it.[3]

---

[2]Beethoven reportedly had a huge dislike for child prodigies, and it took a lot of coaxing from Czerny (who was Beethoven's student) to agree to listen to the young Liszt. According to Liszt's account, he presented a short piece by Ries and, upon Beethoven's request for a Bach fugue, the C Minor fugue from the *Well-Tempered Clavier*. When Liszt was able to transpose the fugue at once into another key, "a gentle smile passed over [Beethoven's] gloomy features." Encouraged, the young Liszt requested to play one of Beethoven's pieces — the first movement of the C Major concerto — which impressed the old master. See Walker, pp. 83–84.

[3]See Cecilia Dunoyer, *Marguerite Long: A Life in French Music 1874–1966* (Bloomington, IN: Indiana University Press, 1993), p. 95.

Hence, *le jeu perlé* was the result of an intersection between the Paris Conservatory, demands of the increasingly played French repertoire, and pedagogy derived from the distinct French light-action Pleyel and Érard pianos (these were still used up until World War I).

LL: And was this intersection between pedagogy, music institutions, repertoire, and instrumental choices also relevant to the development of other techniques in other national schools?

CY: Yes, but I'd add that in the case of some national schools, the influence from external musical figures and lineages would prove very significant to how their playing styles and technique developed. Take Liszt. He might have been rejected by the French school, but he would end up having a major influence on the Russian school through the Rubinstein brothers. The young Anton Rubinstein was deeply impressed upon hearing Liszt in Paris (after being himself rejected admission to the Paris Conservatory in 1840) and his brother Nikolay Rubinstein approached Liszt more than once for faculty recommendations of the Moscow Conservatory. Liszt also influenced the music of such Russian composers as Borodin, Balakirev, and Scriabin and through his virtuosic performances in Russia in the 1840s, dramatically expanded conceptions of what a modern piano could do in a large hall, leading to the development of techniques in the use of arm and body weight. Notably, Rachmaninov became a major figure who continued Liszt's tradition under the tutelage of Siloti (who studied piano with Liszt for three years in Weimar, and harmony with Tchaikovsky) at the Moscow Conservatory.[4]

---

[4] For more details on Liszt's influence on the Russian school, especially on the Moscow Conservatory, see Konstantin Zenkin, "The Liszt Tradition at the Moscow Conservatoire," *Studia Musicologica Academiae Scientiarum Hungaricae*, 42 (1/2) (2001).

So even though Liszt founded no school and passed down no system of technique — he referred to technique as "dirty laundry" that the student should not bring to class — he and his prolific following (once recorded as 400 students, none of whom he charged a fee[5]) undoubtedly influenced the lineage of numerous other schools, including the German and American schools; the same can be said of Leschetizky, who was also a student of Czerny and taught in Vienna and St. Petersburg. In some senses, they had already begun a cross-fertilization of ideas and techniques between national schools before it would fully take force starting from the mid-twentieth century with the breakdown of national barriers — as seen in the emergence of international competitions, education, and faculties — and resettlement due to the Second World War. Today it would be even harder to insist on sticking to the delineation of national schools given the extent of globalization and the proliferation of the media.

LL: So, are national piano schools only of historical interest to the modern pianist?

CY: Yes, in the sense that wholeheartedly adopting national schools of piano technique or playing to guide your pedagogy and inter-pretation would restrict your all-round musical understanding and technical development. You must also bear in mind that so-called national styles of playing are, in the first place, not homogeneous within a single school: Kenneth Hamilton men-tions a rather amusing account of realizing, after his concert in St. Petersburg, that the comment "You play like someone from the Moscow Conservatory" was not meant as a compliment![6]

---

[5]This was documented by Carl Lachmund, an American student who studied with Liszt between 1882 and 1884. Refer to Appendix Three in *Living With Liszt: From the Diary of Carl Lachmund*, ed. by Alan Walker (New York, NY: Pendragon Press, 1995).

[6]Hamilton, p. 12.

In addition, don't forget that today we have access to such a tremendous amount of repertoire, and audiences, too, have developed tastes different from decades ago; the palette of touch and colors expected from the performer is vast and varied.

But also, no, because such knowledge can greatly enhance our understanding of a piece in terms of its historical context and desired sound, which can shape our eventual interpretive decisions.

LL: Can you give me an example of how such knowledge can inform our understanding of the technical requirements of a specific piece?

CY: Suppose you're working on Debussy's *Images*. Knowing the instrumental choices and associated techniques of the French school may give you an idea about the sound Debussy had in mind. While Debussy played on both Pleyel and Érard pianos, he most favored the Blüthner piano which had a fourth "Aliquot" unstruck string that ran parallel to each string trichord, serving only to resonate sympathetically and enhance the overtones — an aural element that cannot be overstated in Debussy.

Further research into the sensitive control of the pedals might enhance your palette of tone colors. While many may associate Debussy's music with a wash of pedaled sound, he had strong ideas about how to use the pedal sensitively, and specifically looked to Chopin (who was the teacher of his teacher, Mme Mauté de Fleurville) for ideas. In a letter to Jacques Durand in 1915,[7] he expressed disdain for pianists who used the pedal to cover up a lack of technique, and instead advocated practicing without the pedal, and even in performance, not

---

[7]François Lesure and Roger Nichols, *Debussy Letters* (Cambridge, MA: Harvard University Press, 1987), pp. 301–302.

holding it on except in very rare instances. The pedal was "a kind of *breathing*" he said, very much echoing Chopin. In addition, he recommended depressing both the *una corda* and the sustaining pedal before playing the first note to achieve immediate vibration of overtones; this could be pertinently relevant to the *Images*.

Lastly, learning how Debussy and others in the French school utilized the drop to create, for instance, the sound quality of the bells as heard in the opening of "Reflets dans l'Eau", might refine your control and manipulation of the range of sounds this specific technique can achieve. "Keep your left hand hanging loosely from your wrist. Then let it drop and let the tip of your third finger play those notes," Debussy advised his student Dumesnil. The use of the drop might strike you as rather surprising given that Debussy envisioned producing the sound of a piano without hammers!

5.3 Damaging Your Tool

LL: You mentioned that circumstances today have given rise to pianists of a more global perspective or exposure rather than pianists strictly adhering to a specific national school or pedagogy. In this respect, would you also say that knowledge on how to practice and perform injury-free have also become more widespread? I'm thinking, for instance, about Scriabin being prescribed "bathing in the Black Sea" and "a diet of kumiss" (a product similar to kefir but containing 1%–3% alcohol) after suffering chronic pain in his right hand from over-practice.[8]

---

[8] Eckart Altenmüller, "Alexander Scriabin: His Chronic Right-Hand Pain and Its Impact on His Piano Compositions," *Progress in Brain Research*, 216 (2015), p. 206.

CY: There was limited knowledge about what to do with musicians' injuries and pains before the field of musicians' medicine was established about three decades ago; musicians back then were regularly prescribed a medley of analgesics, massage, and even electricity. For instance, focal dystonia — a debilitating condition in which the musician experiences a loss of coordination and motor control, typically manifested as involuntary cramping of the hand of curling of the fingers — was largely seen as a psychological or emotional problem from the late nineteenth century. Today, we know that it is a pathological problem in the circuitry of the nervous system, frequently triggered by increased practice, attempts in new technique, change of instrument, or such trauma as fractures or burns. Although statistics show that it typically targets professional musicians, with the average age being 35[9] (afflicted pianists include Leon Fleisher, Gary Graffman, and possibly Glenn Gould in the last five years of his life[10]), it can affect any pianist, including young and healthy teenagers.

This means that teachers and performers should be especially careful when they or their students reach a stage where they might be predisposed to these risk factors. In fact, Scriabin suffered from his injury during a practice spell in which he repetitively tried to perfect strong octave passages and tenths which were evidently too strenuous for his hands. Thus, any increase in the intensity, duration, and type of practice should be closely observed and mapped correspondingly to breaks in

[9]Richard J. Lederman, "Dystonia in Musicians" in *Physical and Emotional Hazards of a Performing Career*, ed. by Basil Tschaikov (London: Harwood Academic Publishers, 2000).

[10]Frank R. Wilson, "Glenn Gould's Hand" in *Medical Problems of the Instrumentalist Musician*, eds. by Raoul Tubiana and Peter Amadio (London: Taylor & Francis, 2000).

practices, alternation in types and intensity of exercises within a practice session, muscular relaxation and strengthening (remember that there are many exercises you can do away from the piano), gradual stretching, and immediate cessation in the event of pain. In this respect, the musician can, once again, learn a few things from the athlete.

LL: Can you give me some specific examples?

CY: It's taken for granted that athletes ought to warm up and cool down properly to avoid injury caused by sudden exertion of muscles. The same strategy, in combination with good posture, reliable technique, and stable practice duration, can also help pianists avoid various musculoskeletal problems especially if they are plunging into strenuous pieces.

Secondly, we often observe athletes going through exercises that seem, at first sight, divorced from their actual sport — take, for instance, our previous example of table tennis players balancing on gymnastic balls. The musician can also learn to develop supportive, auxiliary physical aspects that are, in fact, fundamental to strengthening their overall physique. For instance, a young pianist gearing up for his or her first big competition might never have undertaken any prior feat requiring the same amount of stamina, concentration, and exertion. In this case, slowly increased practice could potentially be supplemented with low-load physical exercises and sports to build up postural back muscles in preparation of the sustained exertion.

LL: Have you personally experienced injury in your career?

CY: It happened to me quite early in my career during a series of performances, sometime in the early 60s. It was a gradual loss of control: I would want to play an octave, only to end up with a seventh. As a young performer with a whole battery of performances your first instinct is to practice more, harder;

even the teachers intuitively thought so. It was costly. At my worst, I could not pick up a comb.

During the search for treatment, I met a doctor from China who managed almost to put me back on track again; I could completely relax the right hand, release all the tension and restart the practice. However, it was at that point that I agreed to play two concerts back-to-back. Disastrous. I realized at that point that my professional performing career had reached a standstill.

As a professional pianist you have a sense of responsibility to deliver at a certain level; when you have a debilitating and utterly unpredictable injury like this, your level can sometimes plummet. It was a difficult realization that performing at the same level was not going to be that possible any more. It was at this juncture that I decided to fully immerse myself into the teaching mentality. This was a natural move to me — I have been teaching from a very young age and have always enjoyed it.

It was in my career as a teacher that I thoroughly learnt about injury prevention, good practicing habits, and the importance of forming reliable technique. Perhaps I, like many other colleagues, could have prevented the injury from taking full reign by intervening much earlier, recognizing risk factors and putting in prevention measures. Hence, it is my aim to pass on this knowledge to my students and other musicians to safeguard their abilities and futures; dirty linen technique may be, but it forms the very vanguard of your success and destruction.

Chapter 6

Let the Pianist Speak

6.1 Taming the Beast

LL: We've talked about many aspects of learning and playing the piano: phrasing, ornamentation, interpretation, pedagogy, and technique. However, taking the next step to perform the piano in front of an audience seems, to me, a rather daunting leap: such concerns as performance anxiety, memory work, and managing stress come into play. What advice would you give prior to taking this daunting step?

CY: Let's first reinforce the positive aspects. Above all, increase your confidence: have a solid grasp of your technical abilities and be assured of your own musical interpretation. Know precisely what you are going to do in each corner of a phrase — leave no room for gray areas. When you're onstage, you're the best: show your strengths and do not be apologetic about the details that you cannot deliver.

Second, cultivate your connectivity with the audience. This depends on a few factors; above all, the character of the performing space. How are you going to persuade the listener to listen to you? If you're in a small room, you can possibly exploit very sensitive nuances of soft, tender sounds, but in a big hall, your contrast would have to be more exaggerated. Or if you're playing in a church, you might need to pedal less or adjust your fast tempi given the resonance of the space.

Third — and this is more a state of mind — remember that you're onstage with a passion to share something. Let this conviction of delivering a message or of communicating a certain emotion lead your performance. Indeed, relish this special occasion in which so many people are gathered to listen to you; allow your imagination and feelings free reign to convey the music as if you were encountering it for the first time. It is this precious, delicate contact with the music that you want to bring the audience through.

Reinforcing these positive aspects often go hand in hand with working through those that are negative. For instance, some performers may feel tremendous pressure because the stakes are too high — perhaps they do not want to disappoint someone in the audience, or they consider that performance the culmination of their achievements. In such cases, the belief that they have something to lose cripples them.

Overcoming such anxiety is usually a protracted, ongoing process, but there are good strategies that can significantly reduce it. For instance, I always encourage my students to enjoy the process of conveying the musical journey onstage; the importance of this cannot be overstated. With secure, controlled and precise preparation beforehand, the pianist can afford to indulge in the moment and allow him or herself to be moved by the music — after all, if you're not moved, how can you move the audience? Once you're entirely in performance mode, it is easier to let go of external pressures and completely focus on the music; whether the audience claps is no longer a priority.

LL: Is performance anxiety a common issue among performers? Did you personally experience it?

CY: I think every musician feels anxious or excited before a performance. Being committed to your art comes with a sense of responsibility and conviction; you want to be in your best form to communicate the composer's message to the audience. In fact, Pablo Casals sees this commitment as a force he cannot escape, almost a subjugation. The story goes that he once went hiking at Mount Tamalpais when a boulder came smashing down on his left hand; he looked at the bloody mess and thought "Thank God I will never have to play the cello again." Making sense of the relief he felt, Casals — who experienced "dreadful anxiety" before each performance — added that "dedication to one's art does involve a sort of enslavement."[1]

Battling with performance anxiety is common, even if you might feel naturally drawn toward performing. I remember feeling a strong affinity to the stage since a young age: singing, acting, playing the piano. I enjoyed having the platform to express, and found it especially heartening to share the occasion with like-minded individuals in the audience and onstage. Then, something happened in my early teens — I had the opportunity to perform at the Victoria Concert Hall, arguably the Mecca of Singapore then. This was how it went: I walked onto the stage gingerly with the unfamiliar lighting shining at me, shrinking me to how a bat must feel when caught in the light. The 9-foot Steinway was not at all friendly: it had a heavy touch and stiff pedals. I started playing but the sound disappeared quickly, making it very difficult to hear myself; all this while, my feet were fashioning some solid tap dance moves due to the disorientation I found myself in. I came through the night solely on confidence and tactile habit. Surely not an

---

[1] Albert E. Kahn, *Joys and Sorrows; Reflections by Pablo Casals as told to Albert E. Kahn* (London: 1970), p. 105.

experience to savor! I told myself that I had to find ways to turn the tables if I were to continue my liaison with the stage.

Since then, I've experienced excitement and a sort of positive, nervous energy before performances, but seldom again anxiety that cripples or debilitates me. However, young musicians who find themselves struggling with stage fright should realize that performance anxiety is very common, even among established artists. Richter, for instance, talked about numerous occasions in which his "heart was beating wildly" and he "almost died of stage fright." On the only occasion in which he conducted — Prokofiev's Symphony-Concerto op. 125 (then titled Cello Concerto No. 2) with Rostropovich as the soloist and Prokofiev listening in the audience, in 1952 — he emerged onto the stage feeling "cold all over" and so disorientated that he stumbled against the podium, leaving the audience in gasps. Funnily enough, this caused his anxiety to evaporate.[2]

And not to forget dear Chopin, who vastly preferred playing for friends in intimate setting to concert-giving. In his biography of Chopin, Liszt recounts Chopin's gripping fear of audiences and public performances: "I am not suited for concert giving; the public intimidate me; their looks, only stimulated by curiosity, paralyze me; their strange faces oppress me; their breath stifles me . . . ."[3]

LL: I've read that Richter preferred to perform only with a lamp by the piano to illuminate his scores in his later decades, keeping much of the hall and himself in darkness. Did you have a chance to hear him play in person?

CY: I heard him in the Salle Gaveau in Paris in the 60s, very late one evening by candlelight. It seemed the concert might

---

[2] Monsaingeon, p. 88.
[3] Franz Liszt, *Life of Chopin* (Massachusetts: 2006, first published 1863), trans. by Martha Walker Cook, p. 46.

have been organized on short notice, which explained the rather extraordinary circumstances we found ourselves in. He played Schumann's *Abegg Variations* — unforgettable. The music, setting, and atmosphere made for a most intimate yet electrifying performance.

Performers come in all personalities; Arthur Rubinstein, for instance, created such a warm, genial persona that just his appearance onstage drove audiences crazy. They wouldn't have cared at all if he dropped a few notes here and there! It was his overwhelming aura and ability to convey music with such a wide palette of colors and emotions that convinced such different audiences. For his later concerts, there wasn't even a need to specify what he was playing; it was simply announced "Rubinstein plays." And yet, he too suffered from performance anxiety. In the photo spread of *Life* magazine, 2 March 1959, you'd see a photo of Rubinstein nervously warming up his hands by the radiator backstage. And below the photo is the caption: "Fear before each concert is the price I pay for my superb life."

6.2 When Things Go Wrong Onstage

LL: Having talked briefly about reinforcing the positive aspects and working through the negative aspects of performance, I want to go into the practicalities of coping with unexpected circumstances during the performance itself. Say I have a memory slip and my mind freezes. What do I do?

CY: Improvise and find a way to go on. Whatever it is, don't repeat the notes, don't correct, don't stop, and don't think back. Easier said than done! I once listened to a pianist who got lost in the same passage five times, but each time she did something different — emphasized an inner voice, projected different dynamics, varied the articulation of certain phrases. Eventually she got out, but the listener almost feels a sense of regret that it's over.

To make mistakes is human; it is the ability to keep the music going under various unexpected circumstances that makes a performer. This ability might come as a natural talent to some, but it can also be cultivated, in part, through practice. But before you work on this, it's more important to first reinforce your memory work as the two generally work in tandem.

LL: What are some strategies to strengthen musical memory?

CY: There are four main aspects to musical memory: musical understanding, physical memory, aural perception, and visual memory.

The first and most important is musical understanding. Study the score, break down its structure and themes, thoroughly analyze its harmony and form, utilize all your background knowledge to further deepen the understanding, leave no measure unturned — you've already seen what such an undertaking might resemble with the short analysis of the Chopin mazurka we did in Chapter 3. A lot of this can be done away from the piano. You must achieve such a thorough comprehension of the piece that you know every single step of the journey — in later stages when you do go blank during a performance, having this secure knowledge of the piece often enables you to improvise toward the next nearest "stop" in the journey to continue playing. In addition, such a thorough analysis would also alert you to the traps that can ostensibly happen in your performance; if you have a Schubert sonata that rechurns its theme numerous times with very small differences, it would help to already be aware of these now and clearly differentiate each appearance.

The physical aspect of musical memory is also quite important. When you play a piece, the notes must intricately link to your entire physical coordination — your finger and hand movements, your feet and pedaling patterns, your sense of balance, and some additional features such as cross-hand passages. This physical memory, or more specifically muscle memory, gives you momentum in a performance to keep going; if you have a memory lapse that leaves you "out of the music" — for instance if you start fearing that you will forget the music a few bars down — pure physical rhythm can sometimes help you tide over briefly until other aspects come into play to help you reenter the music. However, it is best not to rely completely on it as a small slip can easily derail you.

And lastly, you must learn to utilize the aural and visual aspects of the music. The former refers to your perception of sound and aural patterns; if the connectivity of sound and notes is ironclad, this is an enviable form of memory. Some musicians, in turn, have such excellent photographic memory that memorizing music is never a challenge. Arthur Rubinstein used to say that when he plays, he turns the pages in his mind and can even see where exactly the coffee stains are.[4]

LL: And in our practice, do we also try to improvise whenever we have a memory slip to mimic performance circumstances?

CY: You must put in place different measures for different stages of practice. In your initial stages of practice, you should pause when you have a memory slip and try to mentally trace back the music. Ask yourself: What went wrong? Can I recall what should come next? Once you've done this, immediately reach out for the score and put yourself on the right track. You must override your doubts with a firmly corrected version of the music. Do not try the music again before looking at the score.

In the middle stages of practice, the same thing may happen again. This time round, attempt to correct yourself on the piano before checking the score again. It is very hard to forget

---

[4] Harvey Sachs, *Rubinstein: A Life* (New York, NY: Grove Press, 1995), p. 354.

something that you have learnt wrongly; memory work should always be reinforced positively. And finally, in your rehearsal stages, you should simulate performance conditions and play through your lapses without stopping.

There are also numerous strategies a student may find useful to strengthen musical memory. For instance, make yourself start in different places of a work: Can you hear, play, or see what comes next? How about practicing with your eyes closed, as Claudio Arrau routinely did, or in the dark like Mindru Katz? These are all useful tactics to strengthen different aspects of your musical memory.

And if, despite all these, you still have a slip in your performance, don't worry! Perhaps like Richter's stumble on the podium, this slip — not necessarily audible to the audience — will evaporate your anxiety and allow you to convey the music with even more boldness. Correct notes are good, but they can barely be said to make a convincing, moving, or outstanding performance.

6.3 The Curse of Liszt?

LL: All this talk about securing memory work and how to reduce the stress of experiencing a disastrous memory slip just makes me wonder why classical musicians are expected to memorize their entire program as a soloist; after all, such expectations are not placed on chamber musicians, orchestral musicians, or conductors. Given that a large proportion of performance anxiety stems from memory, why not just do away with this convention altogether?

CY: Classical pianists, in fact, used to be met with disapproval if they played from memory. When Clara Schumann played from memory for a concert in Berlin in 1837, Bettina von Arnim reportedly remarked, "How pretentiously she seats herself at the piano, and without notes, too. How modest, on the other hand, is Doehler, who placed the music in front of him."[5] Both Chopin and Beethoven also looked upon playing from memory rather disapprovingly, believing that it might result in the performer paying less attention to detailed markings and expressions in the music.[6] This, coupled to the fact that pianists were routinely seen at the piano without a score only when they were improvising, made performing from memory still a rarity in the early decades of the nineteenth century.

However, by 1840, Liszt had coined the term "recitals" to refer to his solo piano concert in Hanover Square Rooms, London; up till then, pianists were part of mixed concerts with other instrumentalists (Chopin had to share the stage with an orchestra, a singer and a ballet for his first public appearance in Vienna in 1829). This move toward the pianist as the center of attention — in a letter to Princess Belgiojoso, Liszt mentioned that his solo recitals were a way of telling the public: *Le concert, c'est moi!*[7] — gradually gave rise to the image of the soloist as a virtuoso. And naturally, memorizing the whole program dovetailed with this spotlighting of the soloist — not only did it erase physical reminders of the music and the composer performed, it flaunted the somewhat extraordinary capabilities of the performer's memory. Liszt memorized half of his recitals in the 1840s, putting in a place a tradition that would become commonplace by the late 1880s.

To make matters worse (i.e., for expectations placed on future generations of classical pianists), Liszt was not just any other classical pianist; he was flamboyant, mesmerizing, theatrical, sleek, utterly virtuosic, seen either as demonic or godly. He

---

[5] Nancy B. Reich, *Clara Schumann: The Artist and the Woman* (Ithaca, NY: Cornell University Press, 2001), p. 271.
[6] Hamilton, pp. 77–78.
[7] Walker, p. 356.

was a cult. Take a look, for instance, at a review of Liszt's first performance in St. Petersburg, 8 April 1842, given by Vladimir Stasov, one of Russia's most respected music critics then:

Just at that moment Liszt [...] walked down from the gallery, elbowed his way through the crowd and moved quickly toward the stage. But instead of using the steps, he leaped onto the platform. He tore off his white kid gloves and tossed them on the floor, under the piano. Then, after bowing low in all directions to a tumult of applause such as had probably not been heard in Petersburg since 1703, he seated himself at the piano. Instantly the hall became deadly silent. [...] As soon as he finished, and while the hall was still rocking with applause, he moved swiftly to a second piano facing in the opposite direction. Throughout the concert he used the pianos alternately for each piece [...]. We had never in our lives heard anything like this; we had never been in the presence of such a brilliant, passionate, demonic temperament, at one moment rushing like a whirlwind, at another pouring forth cascades of tender beauty and grace.[8]

Liszt became the epitome of the solo piano virtuoso who played every note from his heart — indeed, who was capable of reciting every piece with rhetorical brilliance. From then on, playing from memory has become a mainstay in solo classical piano music; there have, of course, always been notable exceptions, such as Vladimir de Pachmann, Myra Hess, and Richter in his later years.

LL: And what about expectations of the pianist's program? Did that also change alongside expectations of the pianist as virtuoso?

CY: Many factors came into play that significantly shaped the soloist's program to resemble what we are familiar with today: changes in the format of the concert, the artist's dedication and integrity (for instance, they might have strong opinions on performing contemporary music), the expectations of the

---

[8]Walker, p. 376.

audience, and box office targets. When Clara Schumann first arrived in Paris in the 1830s, she was dismayed at the music recital scene, which sometimes consisted of several pianos (up to ten!) played four hands, interspersed with comedy or theatrical acts.[9] Even when Beethoven symphonies were put up, undemanding vocal acts littered between the movements were deemed normal and necessary to help the audience's attention span.[10]

It was not until the 40s that Clara Schumann felt she could finally move away from what she called "the whole world of mechanical virtuoso showpieces" such as those by Herz, Pixis, Henselt, and Thalberg, and the arrangements and variations of other works including those she wrote herself; instead, works by Bach, Beethoven, Chopin, Mendelssohn, Mozart, Schubert and of course, Robert Schumann (even though she was cautious in introducing them gradually to the public), started to dominate her repertoire. Together with Mendelssohn, who was significant in raising standards of programming and reviving interest in the works of Bach, Clara Schumann played some Bach works that had never been heard at the Gewandhaus.[11] Her typical program during this time would consist of a large composition by Schumann or Chopin, or sometimes a less familiar piece of Beethoven (it has been documented that she introduced the op. 101 and 81a for the first times in Leipzig),[12] balanced by smaller works of Mendelssohn, for instance from his *Lieder Ohne Worte* (of which the fifth book is dedicated to Clara).

---

[9] Pamela S. Pettler, "Clara Schumann's Recitals, 1832-50," *19th-Century Music*, 4 (1) (1980).

[10] John Gould, "What Did They Play? The Changing Repertoire of the Piano Recital from the Beginnings to 1980," *The Musical Times*, 146 (1893) (2005), p. 61.

[11] Reich, p. 255.

[12] Pettler, p. 76.

LL: And how did things continue changing in the later decades of the century into the twentieth century? After all, Liszt retired as a concert pianist in 1847, and the latter half of the century saw the rise of other great performers such as Anton Rubinstein and Hans von Bülow.

CY: By the 1870s, tastes and expectations had changed considerably to make programs that balance virtuosity, sensitivity, solidity, and variety a mainstay. More thought was also given to the ordering of the pieces in terms of chronology, weight, and tonality. For instance, Hans von Bülow's recital on 4 November 1875 in New Haven consisted of (in addition to two songs by Lizzie Cronyn, who sang in most of his concerts in the States)[13]

J. S. Bach	*Chromatic Fantasy and Fugue*
	Gavotte in D Minor
Beethoven	*Sonata in E-flat Major, op. 31 no. 3*
Mendelssohn	*Variations Sérieuses op. 54*
	Four Songs without Words 19, 21, 34, 3
Liszt	*Venezia e Napoli*

Compare this to Liszt's Hanover Square Rooms program in 1840, which, in addition to the performer's own compositions, predominantly featured his transcriptions of other composers' works.

Beethoven	*Scherzo, Storm and Finale* from
	Sinfonia Pastorale
Schubert-Liszt	*Serenade* and *Ave Maria*

---

[13]Concert program taken from digital archives of Gilmore Music Library, available at https://www.library.yale.edu/musiclib/exhibits/chopin/hans_von_bulow_program.html

Hexameron	*Fantasia with Variations on the air,* *"Suoni la tromba"* from *I Puritani* by *Chopin, Thalberg, Liszt, Czerny, Döhler,* and *Pixis*
Liszt	*Venezia e Napoli* *Grand Galop Chromatique*

Noticeably, the transformations of the solo piano repertoire also reflected the changing status of the performer from a composer to an interpreter. This led to further specializations in the program offerings, such as concerts consisting of single composers — of which Beethoven has proven to be the most popular over time — or single musical forms. Of the latter, Rachmaninov has offered a concert consisting only of fantasias, and another in 1919 in the Elmwood Music Hall in Buffalo, of 21 *études* by Chopin, Schumann, Scriabin, Liszt, Rubinstein, and himself.[14]

LL: I read that Hans von Bülow was so wildly received that he once had 24 curtain calls for a concert in Leipzig in 1872.

CY: He was bold for his times, pioneering specialized single-composer concerts as an exceptional pianist and conductor. In 1878, he played the last five Beethoven sonatas in an evening, an undertaking unheard of for its time. He would supplement this with a four-fold cycle in 1886, and a further two in 1888, completing the Beethoven sonata cycle in a decade.[15]

But speaking of the Beethoven sonatas, did you know that the young Saint-Saëns, at the age of 11, offered to play any

---

[14] The concert program is available on eBay. Retrieved 25 Jan 2019. https://www. ebay.ie/itm/RARE-Music-Concert-Program-Sergei-Rachmaninoff-Piano-1919-Buffalo-NY-Elmwood-/264065470273

[15] Kenneth Birkin, *Hans von Bülow: A Life for Music* (Cambridge: Cambridge University Press, 2011), p. 335.

Beethoven sonata that the audience requested for the encore? Apparently, he repeated this feat for a subsequent concert when he was well over sixty![16]

LL: That's truly quite a feat — a streak of genius, excessiveness, an extraordinariness beyond comprehension . . .

CY: All good performers are crazy to some extent. I remember that Rudolf Serkin once gave as an encore Bach's "Goldberg Variations", with repeats. Or what about Kendall Taylor, who in response to an audience who wouldn't let him go, played the entire second concert program that he had prepared?

Without excessiveness you cannot go very far, yet without moderation you are bound to lose yourself — that's music: passion, imagination, discipline. Finding the balance is, however, a lifetime study.

***

With these words, I switched off the tape recorder, settled into the sofa and took a sip of tea. It's been three hours since we started, and it was time for lunch. I proceeded downstairs with Prof Yu for our meal of steamed fish and vegetables — "I went to the fishmonger this morning; this fish is great Teochew-steamed" — and devoured the meal with usual gusto.

Outside, the orioles were calling, no longer menacingly but elegantly. "After this, bridge?" Prof Yu interrupted my thoughts, looking at me eagerly. "Seriously Prof Yu?! Aren't you tired?" "Young lady, there's no time to be tired, there's always too much to do." Chew, slurp, gulp. "It's been decided, let's eat up and play bridge. After that, we can discuss the next book — I have new ideas. And by the way, you mentioned you had problems with the Beethoven 'Tempest' Sonata? We can go to the piano after the discussion. You see, that ghostly line can be played in so many different ways . . . ."

***

---

[16] Brian Rees, *Camille Saint-Saëns: A Life* (London: Chatto & Windus, 2012).

Index